D0403152

LIVING THE DREAM

LIVING THE DREAM

DOT RICHARDSON
WITH DON YAEGER

FOREWORD BY
BOB
COSTAS

KENSINGTON BOOKS

http://www.kensingtonbooks.com

KENSINGTON BOOKS are published by

Kensington Publishing Corp.
850 Third Avenue
New York, NY 10022

Library of Congress Card Catalog Number: 97-071967
ISBN 1-57566-203-5

First Kensington Hardcover Printing: July, 1997
10   9   8   7   6   5   4   3   2   1

Printed in the United States of America

ACKNOWLEDGMENTS

Thanks Mom and Dad, for your unconditional love, believing in me, and shaping my future. I love you both very much.

To my family of brothers and sisters, Kathy, Kenny, Laurie, Lonnie, Jake, Kim, Leslie and Scott, thank you for all your support. You've taught me what a true family is all about.

For my coaches, Marge Ricker, Ralph Raymond, Sharron Backus, and Kathy Veroni, you have my gratitude for showing me what type of player and person I should be.

To my friend, Tom, thank you for having the vision and integrity to make a difference. You believed in making our dreams a reality, and because of that, tomorrow others will dare to dream.

CONTENTS

FOREWORD

During the summer of 1996, I was honored to host NBC's coverage of the Centennial Olympic Games in Atlanta. During those seventeen days, we witnessed the best in the world compete at the highest level.

Among the trends I watched unfold was the increased interest in women's sports. The fans didn't just flock to traditional women's Olympic sports like gymnastics and track and field. They were there for soccer, basketball, volleyball, and softball, too. And as you looked over the crowds at those women's events, you could see that interest was not confined to women and girls. Men and boys made up a large percentage of the spectators. It was as if we finally saw the first fruits of Title IX, both on the playing fields and in the stands. A generation of women has grown up with a better chance to play sports with better facilities, more encouragement, and support. And a generation of men has learned to view women in sports differently, not as tomboy oddities, but as respected athletes.

It surely helped that sports like softball had players like Dot Richardson. She helped the audience for women's sports grow because she is so genuinely appealing. Most of us have played some softball. Dot happens to play at the highest level on weekends, but she shows up for work at a real job in the real world on Monday. People can relate to that.

It helped, too, that Dot's energy and her pure love for her game was so evident. She played because it was her passion, not for the tremendous money that has changed so much about big-time sports. The way she plays, the reason she plays, is a lot closer to our idealized notions about sports than most of what we encounter today.

One of my regrets from the Olympics is that I never got the chance to interview Dot in person. But even from the studio, I could sense her excitement, as we reviewed the highlights of each game. And when the team won the Gold Medal, I was set to do a live interview with Dot and the team via a remote camera. We got one question into the interview when the energy of Dot Richardson and her teammates took over. I just shrugged my shoulders and let their exuberance take over.

As a sports fan, I'm glad there are stories like Dot's out there. Stories that engage us, not because of marketing or hype, but because of their simple genuineness. Dot Richardson's story is a story you'll love to read.

Bob Costas
St. Louis
February 1997

INTRODUCTION
MY FIELD OF DREAMS

I have always been a dreamer. Whether my dreams were the type that came in the quiet of a night's sleep or as a sudden vision in broad daylight, throughout my life I have often pictured myself succeeding in a variety of wonderous, exciting ways. To this day, I'm still amazed at how fortunate I have been to live out so many of my dreams.

Not all have come true in the exact manner I would have desired. My dream of one day pitching an inning in major league baseball came true enough when I was given the honor of throwing out the first pitch in a 1996 World Series game. I'd hoped to play collegiate basketball at UCLA, and while I succeeded in making the team, I sat on the bench the entire season. In neither case was the outcome precisely what I'd envisioned, but the satisfaction I got from both experiences was certainly enough for me.

On the other hand, some dreams have become reality with startling accuracy. I headed into the Centennial Olympic Games firmly believing that I would hit the very first home run in Olympic softball history, and also that I would hit the homer that captured the gold medal for the United States. Both came to be.

Any dream, mine or yours, will require tireless effort and dedication if the vision is to become a-reality. On countless occasions, my passions for medicine and softball have demanded sacrifice and caused heartache, as the two careers battled to be the highest priority in my life. There have been times when I was convinced that becoming an orthopedic surgeon, while remaining a world class short-stop, were two ambitions simply incompatible. There would come a day when I'd be forced to give up one of them so that the other might be achieved.

Perhaps that is why the Kevin Costner movie, *Field of Dreams,* is one of my favorite films. You may recall the scene in which the young player, Archie "Moonlight" Graham, ponders his future as he stands on the first base foul line. He must decide to either continue with his dream of playing professional baseball, or forsake it in order to rightfully live out his life as a doctor.

On so many occasions I, too, stood on that foul line. One moment I'd be compelled to hang up my glove and focus entirely upon my medical career, and then the next I'd be determined to retake my familiar position at shortstop. Unashamedly, I weep each time I watch Archie step off the field, leaving his beloved sport behind.

So, for Archie, and for all of you, I have one more story to share. It involves a dream that took almost thirty years to achieve.

One evening when I was six years old, I sat mesmerized in front of the television, watching highlights from the 1968 Olympic Games. The impact upon me was immediate. That same night, I had a vivid dream that as I stood on the Olympic podium, a gold medal was placed around my neck.

On July 30, 1996, my most precious of dreams came true.

CHAPTER

ONE

The Dream of Dreams

Now I lay me down to sleep,
I pray the Lord my soul to keep.
If I should die before I wake,
I pray the Lord my soul to take.
And please Father let there be a softball diamond in
Heaven

It was the bottom of the third inning, the United States vs. China for the Gold Medal in the 1996 Olympic Games. There was a runner on first for the United States. I heard the announcer blare, "Up to bat, shortstop, number one, Dot Richardson." It was the last thing I heard. As I stepped into the batter's box, I saw bits and pieces of my life; the events that led up to this moment raced through my mind.

I was in the backyard of our house in Peasenhall, England. Dad and I were playing catch with a baseball, something I was always begging him to do, even then, when I was

3

six. As I reached out to catch one of Dad's throws, the ball bounced out of my glove and hit my mouth, chipping two of my front teeth. My dad ran over, wrapped his arm around me, and carried me into the house, to mom. When mom saw that I had chipped my permanent front teeth, she was furious. I couldn't understand it. They were only teeth. But I had gotten the chance to play catch with my dad, who would later give me my first official spot in baseball as bat girl on my brother's team. To me life was good.

I stepped up to the plate in Columbus, Georgia. The first pitch—low and outside, ball one. The next—high, ball two. Twice before in the 1996 Olympics we had faced China. And twice I had struck out on an unexpected change-up. I rarely strike out, and they had gotten me twice with the same pitch! With a 2-0 count, I knew what was coming next.

In second grade, I couldn't wait until Field Day. That's when the class spent all day competing in races and field events. I was the fastest runner in school and was scheduled for the fifty-yard dash and so was Tommy. A boy that I really liked a lot. When the teacher said "Go" to begin the race, I started running as fast as I could. I was ahead of everyone. When I looked back, I saw Tommy right behind me. I wanted him to feel good and I thought he would if he won the race, so I slowed up. Afterwards, he bragged to everyone about beating me. Little did he know I had let him win. I let up because I liked him. I wanted him to like me.

I collected my thoughts and stepped back into the batter's box. I knew I had to be smarter this time. I told myself to wait on the ball and cut down on my stride—to be patient. I knew those frustrating strikeouts had to have happened for a reason. As the ball left the pitcher's hand, I knew what the reason was. That's one of the great things about sports. If you handle failure correctly, it can be a great teacher.

During Field Day in sixth grade, the final competition came down to Ricky Fountain and me. Ricky was the fastest boy. I was the fastest girl and had beaten every boy but Ricky. The last event was the long jump. Ricky and I were the only two left with the next jump of thirteen feet. I made it, Ricky didn't. Now everyone was out except for me. The rope was then moved to fourteen feet. I remember the teacher saying, ''Dorothy, if you make this jump, then I will make sure that you are in the Olympics.'' I remember it like it was yesterday because I wanted so much, even at that age, to be in the Olympics. And this was my chance. This was the moment I'd been waiting for. I took my mark and sprinted as fast as I could. I still remember taking off on my left foot, jumping, being in the air, floating. Everyone was on the side of the ropes just watching my feet as they landed past it. But I was at such an angle that my feet slipped, I fell backward, and my bottom landed behind the rope. I had just lost my chance at the Olympics. I was crushed. I spent the rest of the day trying to figure out what I could have done to make that jump. I relived every movement in my mind. How could I improve? What could

I do to make the Olympics next time? Would there even be a next time?

I immediately recognized the pitch . . . another change-up! I waited and only one thing went through my mind: "Rip the cover off the ball." I just exploded. I mean I didn't hold back. I rotated as fast as I could and as I extended my arms I saw the ball explode off the barrel of my bat. I had the feeling that it had the distance to go out of the park. The only question was whether or not it was going to be fair. As I ran up the first base line, I slowed down and bent real low so the home plate umpire had a good view.

I watched the ball float over the fence . . . three feet inside the foul pole. My arms instinctively went up into the air. Then they reached up even higher when I realized this could be enough to win the gold! The first thing I heard was not the roar of the crowd but the voice of our first base coach, Margie Wright. She was saying, "Run! Run!" In all the excitement Laura Berg, who was the runner on first base, was so ecstatic that she was jumping up and down waiting to congratulate me. Everyone was going berserk. I was simply DELIRIOUS! I swear my cleats never touched the ground as I ran around the bases. Thinking about it now, I don't think they ever did during the entire Olympic games. It was such an incredible moment. One of those that will last for a lifetime.

I knew that, with the strength of our team, two runs could be enough to win the Olympic gold. Julie Smith and Laura met me at home plate. Lisa Fernandez congratulated me as I passed the on-deck circle. The rest of my teammates greeted me in the dugout. Coach Raymond never wanted those in the dugout to run to home plate after a home run and the Olympics was no exception. We were all going nuts. Suddenly, I noticed the crowd had become silent. I had no idea what was going on. China was disputing the call. I couldn't believe they thought it was foul. I knew it was fair. In fact, I never looked at the umpire's signal indicating fair or foul because I knew it was inside the right field flagpole. Still, everyone for China was out on the field disputing the call. And the China coaches did not look happy. They knew a two-run lead could mean the game. They had to challenge the call. However, the longer the discussion went on, the more nervous I became.

I felt they were hoping the umpire might give them a call because in the previous inning I had made a throw to home plate while one of their runners was coming in. It was a close play. The umpire called China's runner out, even though replays showed later that my throw was late and, I'll admit, the runner looked to have gotten her foot in.

After a ten-minute argument, the umpire signaled that my home run stood and the USA had a 2-0 lead. Everyone went crazy again. The stadium was rocking. I can't remember another time when I got to celebrate the same hit *twice*.

In sport, part of the game is accepting an umpire's call, no matter how hard that might be. Sometimes the calls go your way and sometimes they don't. Sometimes the ball is a foot fair, sometimes a foot foul. But you never want an umpire's decision to determine a game. And you definitely do not want your opponents to feel they lost on a bad call. Instead, you want them to feel the victory was earned.

Hitting the home run won us the Gold, but it ended up being only a small part of that incredible night. There were so many memories that led up to it and continued after. Before we started warming up for the game, I had walked over to the end of our dugout where a lot of people had congregated to get some autographs and take some pictures. I felt it was important to spend this time with them.

Nothing was a distraction—only an inspiration. People immediately started tossing softballs at me to sign. I caught this one particular ball that had hardly any room left on it. The thought that went through my head was that my teammates didn't leave any room. I finally found a spot to squeeze my name in. As I started to write my name, I heard from the crowd, "No, don't sign it!" I looked up and there was Judy Hall, an old teammate of mine years ago when I first started playing fast-pitch softball. She said, "The ball is for you. We want you to have it." I looked more closely at the ball. And started to read the signatures inscribed: Carol Spanks, Joan Joyce, Sharron Backus, Irene Shea, Diane Davidson, Mary Lou Cushing, Bertha Tickey, Stephanie Tenney, Sue Enquist, Snookie Mulder, Diane "Schuie" Schumacher, Kathy Arendsen, Marge Ricker, Robbie Robinson, Jeanne Contel ('69), Margret Dobson ('62), Shirley Topley, Caroline Fizwater ('92), Gloria May ('73), Dot Dobie ('95), and Judy Hall—all of them legends in our sport. They were just a few of so many talented athletes who deserved to be Olympians but who never had the opportunity. After reading the names,

I looked back up at Judy and she said, ''We are proud of you. Now go get the Gold.''

Each signature on that ball and many more that weren't written were true pioneers in the sport of women's softball. People may look at our Olympic team and say we are the pioneers of our sport, but we are not. The true pioneers of our sport and of women's athletics were those women who played our sport when society said it was not right for women to be athletes. They played for the love of it. They were dedicated. They loved it so much, it did not matter how they were stereotyped or what was said about them. When Judy threw me that ball, the past joined the present. It was such a powerful moment that my eyes started to water. That ball was a message they were living the dream through me . . . through all of us. I walked over to our dugout and put the ball into my bat bag. I knew more than ever now that the gold medal was our destiny.

I ran onto the field. I felt like I was floating on air. It hit me! By playing in the Atlanta Olympics, and making it to the gold medal game, I was living the dream of millions of people throughout the world. We were not just playing for the team. We were not just playing for our country. We were playing for all of them. Those who never got the chance. And those who will play in the future. They were all playing through us.

That I hit a home run to help win the gold medal was, in its own right, almost unbelievable. There was definitely some Olympic adrenaline. I have never been known as a home run hitter, and as a result I rarely think about home runs. But during the Olympics, I thought about home runs a lot. In the sixty-game pre-Olympic tour, I had only two home runs during the entire three and a half months. But my home run in the gold medal game was my third in Olympic competition.

We played well through the rest of the game, led by the pitching of Michele Granger Paulos and my best friend, Lisa Fernandez. When Lisa threw the final pitch of the game, a strike, I just stood there for a second or two. To make sure it really was "Strike three, out Three!" Then it hit me—we won! We had done it! Olympic gold medalists! I raced to home plate where Lisa and our catcher Gillian Boxx already were hugging each other in celebration. We all started piling on each other until we toppled over. The doctor in me instantly surfaced, recognizing the potential for injury. I extended my left arm to try to break the fall of the huddle and to take some of the pressure off those teammates on the bottom, so they could breathe. It was funny to think with all that was happening that was my major concern. Their safety became my priority. Everyone was screaming and crying with joy. I couldn't even talk. It was happening. We were "living the dream."

We survived the pile-up without injury thank goodness and by this time, our coach, Ralph Raymond, made his way over to me around home plate. He gave me the biggest hug! And with tears flowing from his eyes he said, "We did it, Tiger! We did it!" My reply: "I told you we'd do it." Then in the distance behind home plate arose overwhelming cheers and clapping. It was the voice of the "Hall of Famers." They were acknowledging Ralph, his commitment to the sport, and to each of them. Ralph, at seventy-two years old, deserved this moment in history.

The tears were just streaming down my face as I turned

to my parents. My heart was bursting with pride: I was proud of the team; proud of our accomplishment; proud to be an American; and proud to be standing before my family sharing it all with them. I yelled to Mom and Dad that I loved them and again reached my arms into the air to embrace them.

The stadium was packed and now in total pandemonium. We got ourselves together and lined up to shake hands with our competitors. You could see the disappointment in their eyes over winning the silver medal. Nevertheless, they demonstrated they were champions; they never gave up. They always expected their best and gave it. I especially wanted to congratulate the shortstop. That morning before the game, she had told me this would be her last competition. Now we embraced and both started crying. I told her she was a great shortstop. She had made her country proud. She then backed up and in English said—''You are the shortstop. You are the one. I have always tried to be like you.'' I will cherish those words, coming from such a great athlete. I will miss her.

It was then that I noticed security guards had circled the field to prevent anyone from getting onto it. Then I heard my niece and nephew. They had made their way through the crowd to the guardrails next to China's dugout. I ran to them but was stopped by the guards. They reached over the railing to try to share in the moment with me. I reached out my hands to them.

You know in your life, when you take certain pictures in your mind—well, this was one of them. I saw the frozen snapshot of a girl and a boy standing next to each other, reaching out and sharing in the same moment. Realizing that no matter how different we are, each of us can achieve our goals if we are willing to work hard. They lived the dream with me, the looks on their faces showing that they were inspired. And would never be the same again. They know now that they too can live their dreams.

We started to return to our third base dugout when the excitement of the crowd went through us, inspiring us to take a victory lap. I couldn't imagine any other place I would rather be. The fans were chanting "USA, USA." It echoed throughout the stadium. You talk about amazing—it was FANTASTIC! We were reaching past the security guards trying to give high-fives to everyone we could touch!

We returned to the dugout and were instructed to go over to the locker room to change into our award ceremony warm-ups. In the locker room the emotions still flowed. Mostly hugs with joyful tears. We had been through a lot together. We had survived and conquered. When I opened my locker, every movement turned to slow motion. In the calmness, a smile appeared—WE DID IT! It doesn't get any better than this. When we were all dressed, ready for the ceremonies, we were led to the right field foul line.

Hundreds of reporters were gathered next to the fence calling to us. I spotted Mike Todd from *USA Today*. I ran and hugged him. He said, "You did it. Your dream happened." I was shocked he had remembered. In Hazelton, PA, before our exhibition games, he interviewed me. During the interview, he asked what personal goals I had for the Olympics. I told him off the record that I dreamt about hitting a home run in my first at-bat, off the first pitch, scoring the first run, hitting a home run in the gold medal game, and the ultimate dream—seeing the team standing on a podium with a gold medal. I made him swear to secrecy because I felt if he didn't write about it—it would be more likely to happen.

I shared the same dream in one other interview with NBC in Normal, Illinois. I never told anyone else except my family. Next I turned and saw Larry Guest of my hometown newspaper the *Orlando Sentinel.* I ran to him and gave him the biggest bear hug. Bill Buckhaulter and him always kept track of my career through the years. We smiled. Then he had me autograph a sheet in the score book of the gold medal game. I wasn't sure why, but I thought it was great that he had kept score during the game. He said, ''Not bad, two for three, with a winning two-run home run.'' I gave him another hug and never stopped smiling. Then I got called over by other reporters. There were microphones and tape recorders everywhere. Larry told me later that other reporters commented how they had never seen an athlete hug reporters before. I wanted to share the moment with everyone.

We got called over to the foul line to line up for the awards ceremonies. The music started and our march to the podium began. China in front, and Australia behind us. Our arms waved to the crowd. Kim Maher, Lisa, and I held up the USA flag. As we marched, the two of them held it high and proud. We made our way over to the medal stand, where I could not hold back any longer. I looked into the stands and straight ahead stood Mom and Dad, and with them Marge Ricker, my first fast-pitch women's major league coach. Then I looked over to the rest of my family and that group of Hall of Famers who had given me the autographed ball before the game. From across the field, I could see the gleam in everyone's eyes. How perfect did God plan this for me. All those important to me were there to share in this moment. I lifted both arms and yelled thank you to each of them. They probably couldn't hear me, but I wanted to say the words.

We all stepped up onto the podium. No one in the crowd had left. Not a voice was unheard. The spirit of the Olympics poured through our bodies. Individually, each one of us received the medal. As my teammates were given theirs, there was so much going through my mind. The flashbacks of the years gone by and the times when I thought that this moment would never happen for me. It just made it all that much more meaningful.

I took a selfish moment to think about what I had been through. I enjoyed recalling the times when people said I was crazy for doing the things I did in pursuit of this dream. My mind started racing through other important moments in my life—the "challenges." All the flights I had taken from one side of the country to the other to play in softball tournaments while in medical school; trying to get people to cover for me during residency so I could try out for national teams; all the rushing through hospitals and airports; staying in the sport longer than most because I love it, and the hope this day might finally come.

I watched as the Olympic officials called the Chinese team to receive the silver. Then they called Australia for their bronze medal. Then everyone stood and our national anthem started playing. My hand was over my heart and the gold medal was around my neck. I could write for years and never be able to fully describe the thrill. But there was nothing like that moment when I watched them begin to raise the American flag above the right field bleachers. That is when I lost it. I could not hold back the tears. I could hear my teammates crying, too, we were trying to sing the words to the national anthem through tears. The whole moment was just this total mixture of pride and humility. We were the chosen few. The fifteen chosen to represent all who dreamed with us. The moment was now and we were living the dream together.

I do not think I have ever stood so straight or cried so hard. Nor have I ever felt so small in such a big moment. I still get goose bumps thinking about it. It was truly Olympic. From the first day when I prayed to God that there be a softball field in Heaven, I had dreamed of this moment. Now, it was everything I had dreamed it would be. And when one reporter asked if the Gold was worth the $300,000 I may have lost by delaying my career as an orthopedic surgeon by a year, the question almost seemed silly. "It was worth that and more," I said. "Much more."

CHAPTER

TWO

Because You're a Girl

Growing up, there were a lot of things I wasn't allowed to do or be a part of for one simple fact: I am a girl. That was frustrating because there was always one thing that came very natural to me, and that was athletics. I was always able to throw, catch, or kick any type of ball and be pretty good at it. It was actually a talent that I knew was a gift from God. I could feel it. Yet there were times when I was a little girl when I asked God why He gave me so much talent in an area with so few opportunities.

The frustration of being as good as the boys but unable to compete with them was made crystal clear when I was only 10 years old. My dad had just retired from the Air Force and we had moved back to Orlando. My brothers Kenny and Lonnie had joined little league baseball and I would go to all their games. One day, while waiting for one of their games to start, I was pitching to them. I loved it. In fact, I often dreamt about one day being a pitcher in the major leagues. Unbeknownst to me, I was being watched.

A coach walked over to me and commented on how impressed he was with my throwing arm. Then he asked if I would like to join his little league team. I couldn't believe it. These were the words I had been praying someone would one day say. But there was only one catch: He wanted me to cut my hair and answer to the name Bob. As quickly as I had gotten excited, I became crushed. I wanted to play, but I didn't want to pretend to be a boy just to get the chance. I told him, "Thanks but no thanks. If I have to hide who I am, I don't feel it's right."

When I asked my mother later why I couldn't play baseball just being me, she told me it was because the boys would feel bad when—not if—I struck them out and that their parents couldn't handle it when a girl struck their son out. I didn't know if she was right or not but it sure made me feel a little better. Her words showed she believed in me and my abilities. It was just the rest of the world that wasn't ready.

But at that moment, I was devastated. The feeling lasted, however, only for about five minutes. My brothers took off to their game. Then I met a friend of mine, Sunday Brown. She was a very talented athlete who was also denied the opportunity to play organized baseball. She and I walked over to a field nearby and started playing catch in the outfield. We had been playing catch for only a short while when a man came running up the right field foul line. I thought he was going to kick us off the field but instead he asked me if I had a few minutes to talk with a coach. I said sure, and started walking with him to the third base dugout. My first thought was, "not twice in one day."

As we walked past the infield, I noticed the players were

20

not boys. They were women. Before reaching the dugout, a woman walked out to meet me and introduced herself. Boy, was I surprised when she said she was the coach of the Union Park Jets. She wanted to know if I had ever played softball. When I told her I hadn't, she informed me that softball wasn't so different from baseball. The ball was just a little bigger. I took a position at third and fielded a few ground balls. It's funny but already I felt like I belonged there.

The coach then called me back over and asked if I wanted to play on her team. Unbelievable! "Of course," I said. Then she asked how old I was. When I told her I was ten, she was stunned. You see this was an Amateur Softball Association *Women's* fast-pitch Class A team. Most of the women on the team were in their twenties. She had a look on her face that I had seen many times before. Before any words came out of her mouth, I just knew another opportunity to play would pass me by. Instead, she said, "Well, let's go see your parents."

As we drove the mile from the park to my house, I prayed my parents would let me join the team. When we got out of the car, I led the coaches to the front door of the house. That just showed how serious this moment was, because we never used the front door except for very formal occasions. I introduced everyone, then just sat down and listened. It was out of my hands. After a number of questions and explanations, Mom and Dad said "yes" with one stipulation. I would have to put my glove up by my face while in the ready position if I played in the infield. "No problem," I said. I guess chipped teeth is one thing, but the thought of having them knocked out is another.

Up until that time in my life, I had felt I was a player without a team. Now I had found a team—or should I say, they had found me. And the best part was I could play as "Dorothy." What happened to me that day showed me that I did not have to compromise who I was and what I believed in, and that talent will be given a chance.

I often wondered why I was the one chosen and not Sunday. She was a good athlete. The next few years provided the answer. Sunday Brown became the first girl to play baseball at the Union Park Downey Little League when Title IX provided the opportunity for girls to play with the boys if they wanted to. Who knows, if softball hadn't discovered me that year, I might have been playing baseball like Sunday. And maybe gunning for the Atlanta Braves instead of the Atlanta Olympics.

Realistically, the dream of playing in the major leagues was shattered the day I noticed how short-lived Sunday's baseball career was. There were no more opportunities for her after little league, whereas mine continued. At ten, I was already a part of the triple A of the major leagues of softball.

I learned early it doesn't matter how old you are—it matters how well you play. I became the starting third baseman and leadoff hitter for the Union Park Jets. I went from never having played softball to hitting off Class A fast pitches in the fifty to sixty miles per hour range. I fell in love with the sport.

Our uniforms were sharp. The colors were red, white, and blue. I remember they didn't have any shorts small enough to fit me, so my mom and I went shopping for a smaller pair. None of the shorts we found had a stripe on the side. The team's official shorts were red and had a thin red, white, and blue stripe down the sides. Mom and I searched everywhere for a similar stripe. But the only one we could find was wider. We bought it anyway and Mom sewed it onto the sides of my new uniform shorts. It didn't matter that they were different. I was proud to wear them because Mom had put the stripes on for me.

Just before the season started, my parents bought me my first glove, a Rawlings. It was beautiful. I call it my first official glove because I had been using my brother's up to that time. Now I was set . . . my Rawlings glove, my new uniform, and my shiny black Kangaroo metal cleats. I remember being so nervous before the games that I couldn't control the butterflies. In fact, it was a ritual to go to the bathroom before each game because the butterflies were out of control. They seemed to multiply the closer we were to game time. Even thinking about it now, I can still feel them. I was so excited to be able to play.

Baseball wasn't the only sport I didn't get a chance to play as a girl. When we lived in New Mexico, my older brother was on a football team. I actually thought about playing that sport. I was nine years old. I knew there was no way they would ever let me be the quarterback or a running back, which would be my favorite positions, but maybe, I thought, they'd let me be the punter. I loved kicking the football. It was something I was pretty good at, too. Coaches and players alike commented on how far I could kick the ball—much farther than any of the boys on the team—but when it came down to making the team, the length of my kicks didn't matter. Instead it always came down to the fact I was a girl.

Mother reminds me of how amazed she was when we lived in England and I was the regular goalie in my older brother's neighborhood soccer game. I was almost eight at the time and remember loving to play. Mom recalls worrying about me getting hurt playing with the older boys but said she realized I must have been good at it or they wouldn't be asking me to play. They accepted me as an equal because I had the ability to play the game. But the opportunity to play on the boys' organized soccer team didn't exist. Coaches said I wasn't allowed . . . because I'm a girl.

When I was younger there were times when I often thought I would have liked to have been born a boy. Not because I wanted to be one. I just wanted the opportunities they always seemed to have. It seemed that boys got to do everything that I wanted to do. And I wasn't able to play for reasons totally out of my control. It didn't seem right that if someone loved participating in a sport and had the talent to do it well they couldn't compete. If you told me I couldn't play because I was not fast enough, or I couldn't hit the ball well enough, or throw it hard enough, maybe I could say okay, I'll work on it. But when you tell me I cannot do something because of my gender, or my height, or my skin color, those are things I couldn't really change.

It didn't seem fair, but who do you complain to? You tell your mom it isn't fair, and she says "I know, honey, but life isn't always fair." The truth is my parents were very supportive. In fact, if it wasn't for them I wouldn't have been able to accomplish what I have. It was my dad who appointed me bat girl for my brothers' baseball team, which allowed me to practice with the boys and develop my skills. My parents recognized the talents God gave me and helped me seize what few opportunities were available. I believe that is why my parents gave me permission at such a young age to play on a women's fast-pitch softball team.

At the end of that first softball season with the Union Park Jets, I was named to the league's All-Star team. The team was going to Tennessee for a big tournament. A week before we were scheduled to leave, I was climbing some trees in the backyard. I had decided the best way to get down was to swing from one of the branches onto an old white Ford parked underneath the tree. Of course, I was barefooted. As I landed on the car, I lost my balance and fell backwards.

As I started to fall, I looked over my shoulder and saw some boards on the ground with nails sticking up from them. I gave an extra effort in the push off from the car and remember feeling that it was a great athletic move to push myself over the boards. I avoided the nails—but instead landed on an old rusty sickle. A sickle is like a machete with a long broomstick handle, used to cut tall weeds.

Immediately, I felt the sense of a cool breeze through my right foot. I looked down and all I could see was blood. The jagged edge had sliced my foot from the ball to the arch. My younger brother Lonnie and his friend helped me into the house. My older sister Kathy then drove me to the hospital. It took fifteen stitches to close the wound. No muscles or tendons were damaged. If I had landed on that sickle any other way, I could have lost a part of my foot. Because of the injury, I had to give up my position on the All-Star team that competed at the big tournament in Tennessee.

Instead, a few weeks later I hobbled my way up to the registration desk for the Orlando Rebels Instructional League. The Rebels were an Amateur Softball Association (ASA) Women's Major Fast-pitch League team. They competed at the highest level of fast-pitch softball. The "Major Leagues" of our sport.

I was the last to arrive at the registration desk. Hundreds of girls were already inside C.L. Varner Stadium. Jean Daves, a Hall of Famer, was taking registrations. Mom filled out the form and handed it to Miss Daves. She glanced at it, and looking up at me she said, "You're too young." To be a part of the camp, you had to be twelve years old and I was still eleven. I felt my heart drop. Mom told her I would soon be twelve.

About this time the head coach and manager for the Orlando Rebels, Marge Ricker, walked over. She gave permission for me to register for the tryout. In later years, she told me she just didn't have the heart to say no to me. I was just standing there, a freckle-faced, scrawny little kid hobbling on one foot with a look of eagerness, wanting so desperately to play.

During the tryout, we were scheduled to go through different stations that demonstrated our skills in the fundamentals of the sport. The objective was to come up with teams that were evenly matched. But the ultimate goal of the instructional league was to teach fast-pitch softball to more girls and develop stronger talent in a "farm club" system for the Rebels.

Throughout the day, I didn't show very much. I could only run on the outside of my right foot because of the injury. In fact, I hobbled around the bases. I did manage to get a good distance on the throwing station but I didn't figure that impressed anyone. I was wrong. At the end of the day, I was chosen for an instructional team.

That night I realized I had been taught a valuable lesson—everything happens for a reason. No matter how disappointed you may get there is something good in store. I was heartbroken about missing the opportunity of playing as an All-Star in Tennessee. But because of the heartbreak, I was now being taught by All-Americans. Time would show that that painful accident was not a tragedy but a blessing for the future. Life can deal us very tough cards but God will not give you anything you cannot handle. At the time it makes no sense, but with time you see your growth.

After the instructional league ended, Mom got a phone call from Marge. They talked for a while, then Mom asked me if I wanted to be the bat girl for the Orlando Rebels. You bet I did! Marge had selected two of us from the instructional league to be bat girls for the following season. It was a girl named Bemmie and I.

I looked forward to spring training. As bat girls, we attended practices. Every Monday, Wednesday, and Friday from six to nine P.M. Bemmie and I mostly picked up equipment, but we also got to play catch and even shagged balls during batting practice. I would watch and study the skills of the players; even today you can see their influence on my style.

The season started on the last weekend of May, and

culminated in mid August with the National Championship. Doubleheaders were played every Friday, Saturday, and Sunday. I tried to be the best bat girl I could be. I would concentrate on using good form and the proper fundamentals when playing catch with the left fielder. And when it was my turn to pick up the bats, I made it a challenge to pick them up as fast as I could. I was proud just to be a part of the Rebels.

But one fine summer evening, the pride of being a bat girl became the pride of being a softball player. During the second game of a doubleheader, we were beating Alabama 10-0 in the top of the sixth inning. Marge turned to Bemmie and me in the dugout and told us we were going into the game. I couldn't believe what I'd heard. At first, I didn't think she was serious. When I realized she wasn't kidding, I asked, "Is it legal?" Marge replied, "As bat girls you are on the official roster. It's legal. You two are going to hit this inning, then Dot, you go to right field. Bemmie, you're in left."

Everything good that could happen to a player in a game happened to me that night. I came up to bat with a runner on second. I got a base hit. The run scored, giving me an RBI. While on first, Marge gave me the sign to steal. I stole second base. When the next batter got a hit, Marge waved me around third. I beat the throw home and scored a run. On defense, I caught a routine fly ball for the first out. Later, I scooped up a line drive that was hit to me, then I threw the batter out at first to end the game. We had won, and I had played in the "major leagues." At the end of the game, Marge brought Bemmie and I back down to earth. "Get off cloud nine and start packing the bats," she said with a smile.

Later that week I wondered why I was put in right field. Maybe Marge put me there because I was not that good. Everybody knows the worst player is put in right field. Or so I thought. When I asked Marge what I needed to work on, she told me, "You must be kidding. The player with the best arm goes to right field." I learned a new appreciation for that position and the talent it requires.

That was the season of 1974. It also was the year the ASA National Championships for Women's Majors was held in Orlando, Florida. The Rebels were the host team. I got to observe the thrill of competition at the highest level. And of course as a bat girl, did so from the best seat in the house. At that tournament I met and got the autograph of Joan Joyce, a legend in her own time.

In the fall, I competed again in the Rebel instructional league. At the end of the season, I was selected for the newly formed Little Rebels, a fifteen and under girls softball team organized and coached by Marge herself. I was thirteen. One week later, Marge pulled me aside from a team meeting. We walked down the left field foul line toward third base and stopped for a minute. When we were far enough away from the rest of the team, she told me she had already spoken to my parents and they'd said the decision was up to me. She said, "Dot, you have the opportunity to play with the Big Rebels if you would like. But before you answer, realize you can stay with the Little Rebels and be a big frog in a little pond, or you can play with the Big Rebels and be a little frog in a big pond."

Without hesitation I said, ''I want to be a little frog.''
I joined the Rebels that 1975 season and at thirteen years
of age became the youngest player in history to play ASA
Women's Major League Division.

Even though I was able to play softball with women
twice my age, there still weren't many athletic opportunities for girls at Union Park Junior High. In fact, I had to
be on the boys track team in seventh grade because there
wasn't a girls team. The next year the school started having
girls sports. When I look at the trophies I was awarded in
Junior High, I am reminded of the evolution I've watched
in sports. My seventh and eighth grade trophies had a male
figure on the top. But by ninth grade, there seemed to be
a little more acknowledgment of women because they had
found trophies with a female figure.

During my ninth grade year, I played four sports: volleyball, basketball, softball, and track. The sports banquet
held at the end of the year was a momentous evening. I
had been selected as the Most Valuable Player in each of
the four sports I played and became the first girl named
as our school's Outstanding Athlete of the Year. There
were four trophies and one beautiful plaque on the table
before me. I remember after receiving the third trophy, I
started hoping one of my teammates would be awarded
the next.

But the school made sure I didn't get a big head. All
the awards I received that night spelled my name D-O-R-
T-H-Y, instead of D-O-R-O-T-H-Y.

By high school, there seemed to be more opportunities
for girls to participate in athletics. I played five sports:
volleyball, basketball, softball, track, and tennis, as well

as continuing to play for the Orlando Rebels. It really wasn't as tough a transition as you might think. Each sport prepared me for the next. And each sport easily became my favorite. At school, we played slow-pitch softball. I couldn't believe we were having to play slow-pitch when colleges were giving scholarships for fast-pitch. I was fortunate that I was playing for the Orlando Rebels.

Some coaches wondered how I managed to play both without affecting my hitting. Well, Marge taught me how to hit left-handed when I was only 12. So for slow-pitch I hit from the right side of the plate and in fast-pitch from the left, therefore I didn't develop any bad habits.

I've always acknowledged the importance of education. It was encouraged in our home. We were taught to always do the best you could in every thing you did. That is the definition of a student-athlete. Not only was I All-Conference in every sport I played but I was also a member of the Junior National Honor Society, National Honor Society, Spanish Honor Society, and Dean's List.

The sports banquet my senior year at Colonial High School was as memorable as the one from my last year of junior high. I received the Most Valuable Player Award for each of the sports I'd played, but the coaches were undecided on how to handle the Outstanding Athlete of the Year Award. Previously it had only been given to a male athlete. My qualifications were unmatched. However, the decision was made to present dual awards to both a male and female athlete. That was seen as a disappointment by those who thought that I deserved the title alone. I was honored by those who'd argued for me. They made it possible for me to stand behind the podium and accept the award with a feeling of pride. It was the same award my older brother Kenny had received just three years earlier. He was in attendance with my parents. That night I was proud to recognize Kenny's accomplishments and his inspiration to me.

As I look back at my participation in sports during high school, it is interesting to analyze my decision not to run track until my senior year. The reason I didn't participate during my tenth and eleventh grades was because I got so nervous. Why? I was afraid of being beaten. Of losing the race. Of not being the fastest. It was so individualized, all my thoughts were about me, and I didn't like it. I put too much value on the result of the race instead of the competition. I grew up during those two years. I learned the importance of the challenge and the attempt to face it, not to hide from it. I learned, too, that your worth as a person does not lie in the win/loss column or in your batting average. Instead it lies within you and the things you do.

I joined the track team my senior year and loved it. I found a sense of security in who I was and the effort I gave, not in what others would think if I lost.

During the summers with the Orlando Rebels, I traveled the country playing softball. Our Rebels team was so incredibly talented that I seemed to learn something every time I took the field. It was like having fifteen mothers. We traveled in a motor home for road trips in the Atlanta Coast League and to Texas. Everyone would take turns as the driver or the copilot. Of course I could only be a copilot since I was too young to drive. I always slept in the bunk over the top of the driver and copilot. It was a small area, but perfect for me.

I remember being so excited about playing the upcoming games that I couldn't sleep at night. I would count the white striped lines dividing the road, the whole time listening to the eight track tapes we kept on the bus. The team favorites: the Stylistics and the Best of Bread, played over and over again. Even today when I hear those songs I can sing every word.

We played against the Stratford Raybestos Brakettes, the Atlanta Loreli Ladies, the Waltham Drifters, the Allentown Patriots, and the Bridgeport Coeds, to name a few. I'll never forget my first trip to play against the Raybestos Brakettes. It would be my first time facing the "living legends." We drove up to this gorgeous stadium, the Raybestos Memorial Field. The parking lot was full and the stands packed with four thousand people. One of the most embarrassing moments in my life happened before that game. As we ran out to take infield I tripped over the shoelaces of my brand-new cleats. I fell to the ground. I got up so fast I doubt anyone even saw me. If you blinked, you would have missed it.

It was that game when I first faced Joan Joyce. You know someone is good when you can remember how you performed against them. I got a hit the first time up to bat against Joyce. When I was on first base I looked in the dugout and every one of my teammates was busting up laughing, mostly in disbelief that this kid had gotten a hit off the legend. I'll never forget it. A hit up the middle. Our celebration was short-lived, however, as none of us touched the ball for the rest of the game. Joyce was a true competitor and she simply decided that my hit would be the last of the evening.

Imagine being on the road playing softball at thirteen years of age. We were given five dollars a day for meal money. Five dollars! That was a lot of money to me. I had never been given meal money before so it was a big deal. It was great but I did some crazy things. I had a chocolate milkshake for breakfast, lunch, and dinner for an entire three weeks on a road trip. When I came back home I had pimples all over my face. I broke out from all the chocolate. Another time I ate six doughnuts for breakfast and couldn't move without feeling sick. Not much nutrition there either.

During that first year with the Rebels, many of the players I admired, like Snookie Mulder and Kathy Stilwell, left the Rebels to form a new team called the Orlando Suns. Their absence created openings in the roster, and that's how I was given the opportunity to become a starter. I was the leadoff batter and resumed my place in right field.

I truly loved my position in the outfield. Warm-ups were especially fun for me, as I had the opportunity to throw the ball to each consecutive base. One night, when I gunned the ball to third on a line shot, everyone in the stands—fifteen hundred people—stood up and gave me a standing ovation. In a warm-up! To me, it was just a warm-up throw, but that is how astonished people were at a thirteen-year-old playing in the women's majors.

After one of my first games, I was asked "How old do you feel when you play?" I said, "I never think of age. It does not really matter how old you are, it matters how well you play." The reporter didn't like my answer and repeated the question. "Ok," I said. "I feel 21."

In 1976, the Women's Professional Fast-pitch softball

league was formed, backed and supported by Billie Jean King. There were teams throughout the country. I was on the protected list of the Connecticut Falcons, though it didn't matter to me. I did not want to play professionally because I wanted to participate in the Olympics. I didn't know when but I knew I wanted it to happen more than anything.

By playing for the Rebels, I was able to be part of the real growth in women's softball. For that, I have to say thanks to that Little League baseball coach who wanted a pitcher named Bob.

CHAPTER

THREE

Stereotypes

I was in seventh grade, twelve years old, when I first heard the words: "You're a lesbian." The shot was being taken at me by one of my best friends during an argument. I asked, "What is that?" I didn't even know what she was talking about. I went home and questioned mom.

When mom explained it, I was crushed. Why did someone who knows me call me that? I said, "I haven't had sex with anybody. How can they say that about me?" Mom said it was probably because I was a girl and an athlete and that's what many people think of girl athletes. That hurt. I was being *stereotyped* as a lesbian in the seventh grade—just because I was athletic.

I learned quickly that dealing with that stereotype was going to be the hardest part of being a top-level woman athlete. It was going to be harder than losing games, more challenging than going through tryouts, more painful than most injuries. Whenever homosexuality was brought up, the connotations were always negative. Hence, whenever

I was called a lesbian, I concluded that it must be something pretty bad. The wound was planted early and deep. It affected me to the point that I found myself becoming less and less affectionate toward people. I feared their heterosexual reputations might be ruined if they associated with me.

When you're young, as I was at the time, the opinions of others drive a lot of your thoughts, a lot of your actions and your emotions. For that reason, I tried out for the cheerleaders in seventh grade, because they were the ones who got all the boys. They were the ones that were thought to be the most feminine. That was how I reacted to the pressure. I was trying to fit in to what everyone thought a girl should be—cheering for the boys. Thank goodness I didn't make it. Because if I had made it, I wouldn't have been able to compete in the four sports I chose to play.

I was on the boy's track team in seventh grade, running the 440-yard dash. I loved the competition, but I hated being thrown on to a boys team, because it confirmed what everyone else was thinking—oh, yeah, you want to be a boy. The truth is, I just wanted to compete. I wanted to play. I've never wanted to be a boy. I've always been proud to be a girl.

But when you're younger, you spend too much time worrying about what you look like, what people think about you. When we moved to Orlando, I had three great friends, Cheryl, Becky, and Ruby. It was always Becky and Ruby who had the boyfriends. The boys thought they were the prettiest of us four. They were taller, more striking. I never considered myself pretty. I even used to think,

"Yeah, I don't blame the guys if they want to date someone prettier."

I did not get many dates in high school, and those that I did were nonathletic guys. Boys seemed to choose their dates by how they make them look. A cheerleader makes them look good. A thin blond makes them look good, and I am not that. I am short, freckled, and very athletic, usually more athletic than they are. Thus, the boys I dated were ones without fragile egos, particularly in athletics.

Sure, I wanted to date the great basketball player, but it was not going to happen. That is hard to deal with, but that whole part of growing up is hard to deal with for almost all girls. It takes time to learn that nobody can give us self-esteem.

In tenth grade at Orlando's Colonial High School, I said I was tired of not going out. I wanted to date. I got asked out to a football game by this guy who had a little acne problem. But I decided I wanted to go out and accepted his offer to go to a football game. It was horrible. He didn't know that I knew a bit about football. So all during the game, he was telling me things about football that weren't right. But I just let him go on, because I was trying to be the polite, feminine date. When we got to my home, he gave me a french kiss and, at the time, I don't think I've ever felt anything more disgusting. I went in and went straight to the bathroom to brush my teeth. That cured me of my *need* to go on dates for some time.

About that time, I started to understand the whole homosexuality and heterosexuality issue. It was then that I learned for the first time that one of my teammates was gay. My reaction was, "That can't be. That's not really sex." I'll admit I was a little freaked out. I made a bunch of errors in the next few games because I was so preoccupied with the situation. I acted differently toward her, and even got angry at her and thought it was players like her that gave me a "bad" name. But what is bad and what is good? Moreover, who was I to judge? What made me better? It was so wrong of me, so childish.

The next year, it hit me. Did it really matter what her sexual preference was? Wasn't she still a good ball player, a good teammate, a good person? I hoped that this new open-minded approach would end the issue for me, but, as you can imagine with something so complicated, it took years for me to get comfortable with the subject.

While I was struggling with the issue, I decided that the best road for me to take was to act naive. I pretended that it didn't exist. It worked, because no one bothered me. No teammate on any team I played for ever said anything to make me feel uncomfortable. In fact, the opposite happened. I was young and on a women's team, so many of my teammates protected me, shielded me from the gay issue.

I got over my personal anxieties enough to become close friends with some of my gay teammates. They didn't give me grief about my choice. I didn't give them grief about theirs.

As I struggled with the issue in my teens, it bothered me when people said bad things about me. It got to the point where if one person said a single bad thing about me, I would focus on that one person as opposed to the 20,000 other people that loved me. I would try to change my life or do whatever I thought was needed to change the opinion of that one person: wear a dress everyday, or wear my hair long—whatever I had to do to try to get that person to know me. Maybe then he or she would stop talking about me.

Junior high and high school was a tough time to face that, when you're going through acceptance and growing pains. Then I realized that it is important to be who you want to be, and people are going to continue to talk if they want to. I learned to be secure in who I am. I am expressing the talent I have been given and loving every second of it.

But that led to one of the most disappointing moments in my life. While in college, one of my best friends told me she was gay. It didn't bother me a bit. But one night, she asked me if I would "consider her sexual views." I knew what she meant. I backed up and said "No way. That's not me." I was just so deeply saddened that someone that close to me didn't understand me. She, too, was labeling me because she knew I accepted her and felt comfortable around her.

I rushed out of my dorm room. I was so hurt that I looked at my dorm neighbors and just said, "If you have a daughter, don't you ever let her compete in athletics, because it's not worth it." That's when I hit the lowest point on this issue. The tears flowed freely as I ran to my car. If someone who knew me this well thought I might be gay, would I ever be accepted as a straight woman?

As I was driving away from the dorm in a torrential downpour, I was crying so hard I could hardly see. I was so hurt that I actually thought about getting into an accident that night and killing myself. Why do I have to put up with this? Why does this keep popping up? What is wrong with me?

Then, all of a sudden my eyes dried. I thought to myself, "You can't let other people drive you to this. You know who you are. You have a talent that shouldn't be wasted because others say things or situations become uncomfortable." It was an incredible moment. I drove the car over to the softball diamond and started jogging around. That was my place of comfort.

My disappointment was in myself, too. I reacted to that incident in all the wrong ways. I think all the time about those words I yelled at my neighbors and wonder if some great young athletic girl, with all kinds of God-given talent, was not playing sports today because her mom, my dormmate, heard my words. If that were true, the cycle will go on and I'm ashamed that I helped it along.

I believe the stereotyping of female athletes as lesbians has been one of the greatest hindrances in the development of women in sports. Parents don't want those things said about their daughters, so they deprive them of the opportunity to express their talent. The girls don't want to have to argue the point. And who can blame them? There are still a lot of ignorant people causing a lot of pain.

Like most women athletes, I have lived with stereotypes about my sexuality, but not as much as the pioneers before me. That is why I admire the women who played early in the sport. They were the true pioneers who stood up and ignored the things that they heard said about them. They had short hair and they played a game enjoyed mostly by men. They played so one day we could play freely.

Unfortunately, society hasn't advanced as quickly and open-mindedly as they had hoped.

People whisper about women athletes. The hard part is that it is said behind your back. You hear the stories about people saying things, but the troubling part is it is never the people who know me. I would hear that someone would say, "Dot is a dyke," or "Dot must be a lesbian." But how did they know that; had they ever asked me?

But the one thing I'm sure of is that I was born at this time so I would know the challenge that successful women face. I can then share those stories with young girls. I feel very strongly that I need to be a motivator, a person who has experienced those tough times and who will not let young girls forget the trials earlier generations endured so that they could play. I know that I am here to try to make things better. I'm willing to deal with the crap so other girls don't have to. If I really thought I could protect my nieces from what I've been through, I'd take twice the criticism I've taken.

However, I'm hopeful that the attention and respect given women's sports in the 1996 Olympics is the reflection of the changes in society. I hope we have developed women's athletics to a point where now society appreciates the talent, no matter what the gender, no matter what race. And that is something to commend . . . the key is that society has got to come to a point where no one cares what your sexuality is. We need to accept people for who they are.

As a doctor, am I supposed to treat one person differently than another because they are black, or they are white, or they are Hispanic . . . or they are Asian, or that one is a homosexual and one is a heterosexual? We have to accept people for who they are. There are homosexuals in sports and there are homosexuals out of sports, and what difference does it make? How somebody wants to live her life is her choice, and we need to, as people, appreciate others for the talents that they have and for who they are.

To pass judgment on somebody else, especially when you don't even know them, shows a simplemindedness that saddens me.

There was a point in my life when I just said, well, I am going to be asexual; I'm not going to hug anybody, I'm not going to let anyone come near me. But the whole thing is, what does sex have to do with it in the first place? I mean, they don't say, "Gosh, she's a woman surgeon, she must be a homosexual." Or, "Wow, she's a woman lawyer, she must be gay." But when it comes to softball and most sports, it is different.

Why should this stereotype exist so strongly in sports? Many suggest it's because there are proportionately more women in sports who are gay than there are in other walks of life. I don't buy that in the least. I think people just say it more about sports.

It might shock people to know that I've never been on a team where even a third of the members have been gay. On most teams, the number was much lower. So why are all of us painted with that brush?

Most of my friends got out of athletics because of the whispers. They either were not getting a lot of dates or boys—or even other girls—were saying hurtful things about them. Or their parents were giving them a hard time.

Everyone, it seemed, was discouraging them from being an athlete. So they quit.

Well, since the Olympics, I've gotten letters and calls from a number of those girls saying, "What if I'd have stayed in it? I was good, wasn't I? Where would I be today? Why did I let society, or a guy, or a group of people take me out of what I was good at and what I enjoyed? Now I regret it." There was that doubt that they would have to live with the rest of their lives, and that's a shame, because they made a decision based on other people's opinions.

I am so glad that God gave me the strength to persevere and gave me the support of my family. My mom and dad have never said that I ought to be married, I should be having kids by now, or that girls do not play softball—or that girls do not become surgeons. My parents have always told me to do what I want to do, do not let anyone change my mind or get in the way, and I would become who I wanted to become.

I think I have become that person. The juggling act of handling my career as a surgeon, my love of softball, and the occasional night out with a date is the equivalent of several full-time jobs. There never seems to be enough time for my personal life, but I don't feel at thirty-five any pressure to change that.

The challenge of surrounding yourself with people who feel the same way is not an easy one. While I was at UCLA, I dated a guy whose company I really enjoyed. He seemed unfazed by my athletic interests until one day when he invited me to play his sport: bowling. I beat him. Then he asked if I had ever golfed before. I said no, so he took me off to a nine-hole course nearby. I tied him. He was furious. He said he wanted to play real golf and took me to an 18-hole course. I don't remember who won, but his attitude about my interest in sports seemed to change.

One day, he said, ''You really don't want to keep playing softball, do you?'' Then later in the conversation he said, ''You don't really want to be a doctor, do you?'' Suddenly I realized he wasn't interested in me being me. He was discouraging me from doing things that I love to do. Those things didn't fit his visions of a mate and he wanted me to give them up. I suddenly realized that this was not the way it was supposed to be. It really hurt me that he wasn't as excited by my success as I was by his. But it taught me an important lesson about friends and mates: The ones who love you want you to achieve everything that you want and those are the ones to hold on to.

There are times when I know that my passion for sports and for my career have cost me relationships. There are times I have regretted that. But I'm still old-fashioned enough to believe that in order for a relationship to be right, it has to be right on all fronts.

I deal with life and death every day in the hospital. I have learned to appreciate life and regard all the rest— what someone thinks of you and your interests, if you are homosexual, heterosexual, black, white, Asian, Hispanic, right-handed, left-handed, short, tall—as trivial. It was not easy to get to that point. Unfortunately, you often have to grow old enough and mature enough to know the real you and be confident in who you really are, not in what others think.

One of the joys that I have in life is knowing when my five nieces were born that they would have an awesome and exciting future. I want them to have as much opportunity as my five nephews do, and I'm willing to do whatever it takes to see that happen.

I know the day is out there when women athletes will be admired for their athletic talent, without the hurtful comments about their sexuality.

FOUR

Rebel Yell

It was August 1981 and the Orlando Rebels had what I believed was the chance of a lifetime. We were playing in the Amateur Softball Association Women's Major National Championship double-elimination tournament, and were in the winner's bracket with the fifteen-time defending champion Stratford Raybestos Brakettes. The Brakettes were so famous that a film crew from *60 Minutes* was there to chronicle the next national championship for this legendary team. I like *60 Minutes,* but I wanted badly to ruin their documentary.

We played in front of a packed crowd in Houston's Memorial Park and, in an amazing game, we won 1-0, sending the Brakettes into the loser's bracket and us to the championship game. The way that works is that the Brakettes, coached by Ralph Raymond, then had to play a game to get to the championship game. If they won, we played again the next day. If they lost, they went home and we played the other team for the title.

We went back to the hotel to wait and find out who our

finals opponent would be and, wouldn't you know it, the Brakettes came through in the clutch to play us again.

To win the national championship, all we needed was one win, and they had to beat us twice. In that first game, though, they beat us in 10 innings, 1-0, on a home run by Diane Schumacher, now in the international Hall of Fame. Her hit forced one final game.

The championship game was fiercely competitive, and in the bottom of the seventh inning, with everything on the line, the score was 1-0, with Stratford ahead behind the pitching of Kathy Arendsen. She was throwing a perfect game heading into that final inning. No Rebel had even reached first base. Kathy was firing her seventy-mile-an-hour pitches from a mound only forty feet away.

I was our leadoff hitter. I remember walking up the steps to get out of the underground first base dugout. A cameraman was in my way so I patiently waited and politely said "excuse me," as I grabbed my bat from the rack. There was a calmness inside me at that moment, an air of confidence and belief. When my name was announced over the speaker as the next hitter, I stepped into the batter's box. In my peripheral vision I saw a man stand and start clapping and then another next to him, then another, until the sold-out crowd of 4000 was on its feet. It broke my concentration, so I quickly stepped out of the box. It was a standing ovation. And it was for me.

I had played one of the best tournaments of my young career, one of those strings of games where mind and body are perfectly in sync. Defensively, I had made plays I don't think I had ever made before. I was making unbelievable stops over behind second base, and a great couple of plays all the way over behind third. I was all over. I knew these Nationals had something magical in store. I could feel it inside. Every time I stepped onto the field I felt I was one with it. From the first game on the team played as one. For me, I felt I was in on every pitch. I was reacting without inhibition and my range even amazed me at times. I was getting a lot of action, with fourteen putouts in one game.

At that moment, I said a prayer to God to thank him for allowing me to be on the field showing the world what he has given not just to me but to all of us. I collected my thoughts and got back into the box. Arendsen had been superb. First pitch, high, ball one. Next pitch, right there and I connected. The ball shot into right center field. I quickly ran to first and rounded the base ready to head for second, but the outstanding backhand play by centerfielder Sue Enquist held me to a single. We had to score. We had to win. We were as close to a national championship as we had ever been. The Orlando Rebels had never won a national championship in the thirty years of the organization. There comes a point in your life when you say I'm giving it everything I have because second is not meant to be.

Behind me in the lineup was Snookie Mulder who, when I was first a bat girl in 1974, was a star for the Rebels. I had always said that with her in the lineup, something magical was going to happen because she's so good. Well, Snookie watched two strikes go by. I was yelling at her, giving her all the support I could when she wheeled on the third pitch, a Kathy Arendsen fastball, and laid down the perfect bunt down the first base line, sending me to second on a sacrifice.

Patti Pyle was next up to bat and was intentionally walked by Kathy because throughout this tournament I would get a hit, Snookie would send me over, and Patti Pyle would drive me in. Everyone else had struck out over and over again against Kathy. Now I was on second with Patti on first.

Jo Ann Ackermann was next up. So far in the tournament, Jo had struck out every time against Arendsen. But this time, Jo hit the first pitch and her slow grounder scooted under the first baseman's glove and into right field. I leapt away from second base and already had my sights set on home plate when Marge called for me to hold up at third. Of course I followed my coach's instructions, but as I held up and watched the ball ever so slowly bounce in toward home, I knew I could have beaten the throw.

But suddenly, the opportunity to score reappeared when the catcher lost her focus and the ball slipped past her glove and to the backstop. There was no stopping me this time as I roared down the third base line. I dove head first into the dirt and felt the coolness of the plate beneath my hands. I looked up through the considerable dust cloud I'd created and saw the umpire emphatically giving the ''safe'' signal. We'd tied the game! My exuberant teammates picked me up out of the dirt and helped me back to the dugout.

The winning run was now on third! I knew down deep we were going to win. Any kind of hit and we would be national champions for the first time in history.

It was now in the hands of Shirley Burton. As she went to the plate, I thought she looked nervous. When she swung at the first pitch—which was a full five feet above her head—I knew she was. But who could blame her? Shirley turned around and looked in the dugout and said, "I'll hit it, I'll hit it somewhere."

Sure enough, she popped the next pitch right up the middle. It bounced over the outstretched glove of Kathy Arendsen. The Brakettes' second baseman, Allyson Rioux, backhanded the ball and fired it home. The throw was up the line. Patti Pyle collided into the catcher, who was trying to catch the ball. They both fell to the ground and the ball went to the backstop again. The next seconds felt like they were in slow motion. Patti was still three feet from home plate and was crawling toward the game-winning score. Patti slowly made her way to the plate and we were yelling, "TOUCH THE PLATE!" I can still picture her lifting her right hand and slapping it down on the plate. And that was all it took. We did it!

When she touched the plate, the umpire yelled "Safe." The crowd started running onto the field. It was, many old timers said, the greatest finish ever in a national championship game.

It was the first time a team from Orlando had won the national championship and it was considered one of the biggest upsets in women's softball history.

Our team drove back to Orlando and when we arrived at old Varner Stadium, hundreds of fans were there to welcome us home. As the crowd walked through the greeting line, I suddenly received a huge hug from a woman I recognized as a one-time Rebel. After her long embrace, she said, "Thanks for doing what none of the rest of us could do. You're an inspiration."

I've thought about that line for fifteen years. It made me realize that while I'm playing a game, I really do have the opportunity to give something back to people through athletics. I realized that there are thousands of other players out there who enjoy the game, just as I do, but who haven't been as blessed with the opportunity to play in games like that one. I've been given a gift and it is a gift most precious when I share it.

And, we ruined a great *60 Minutes* piece.

FIVE

American Pride

As my senior year in high school was coming to an end, the biggest news to hit our sport was announced: Softball would be played at the Pan-American Games in the summer of 1979. The reason this was so significant is that in order to even be considered as an Olympic sport, you had to be included in the Olympic family. By making our game a part of the Pan-American Games, the Olympic Committee was finally and formally inviting us into the family. Softball now was considered a Group A international sport, which meant it was eligible to be a medal sport in the Olympics.

We could only dream that this would one day lead to the Olympics. Four Pan-American games and seventeen years later, we finally made it to the Olympics games.

That I was even asked to try out for the team at age seventeen was, in itself, quite an honor. There were only two ways to earn an invitation; one was to have been an All-American, which I was not that year, or to have been an "at-large" selection. I earned the latter by my performance in the 1978 National Championships, having caught the eye of Ralph Raymond.

It was in the spring of 1979 I learned that I'd have the chance to try out for the team. My Orlando Rebel coach, Marge Ricker, called myself and my teammate Patty Pyle over to her apartment. First, Marge told Patty that as an All-American, she would receive a plane ticket to fly her out to Colorado Springs. Somewhat dejectedly, I sat on her couch wondering why she had called me over. It was then that Marge told me that I'd been given an "at-large" selection, and that I'd be heading to the Olympic Training Center as well as Patty!

Marge paused, then said, "You're not going to make the team, but I think it will be a great experience for you to compete against players at that level. So enjoy yourself."

So just a few hours after my high school graduation ceremony, I stepped on the plane for Colorado Springs. While at the airport, my mom reached over and wrapped her arms around me. Smiling, she said, "Dorothy, something tells me you're going to make this team. Go out there and do your best."

My hope of comparing myself to our nation's finest shortstops was rather short-lived, for on the first day of tryouts I was instructed to take a position at second base. I had never played second in my life! I played right field when I was thirteen, third base for the Orlando Rebels when I was fourteen, and then I played shortstop from fifteen years of age on. Obviously, it was very different. The throw to first base after making a play is a lot closer from second than it is from shortstop. From second, I was winging the ball so hard to the first baseman, Diane Schumacher, that she was ready to kill me. She was yelling "Quit throwing the ball so hard." I did my best to back off, but the adrenaline seemed uncontrollable.

After the final tryout game, the selection committee informed us that the roster would be posted in the main building around six o'clock. I could hardly stand the wait. Finally, as I was walking from the housing barracks down to check the list, one of the players who had tried out approached me on the sidewalk. As she passed by, she quietly said, "Congratulations."

I couldn't believe it, and it wasn't until I saw the list for myself that the reality hit me. I would be representing the United States in the 1979 Pan-American games. It's a moment every athlete dreams about; to wear the red, white and blue, and to have "USA" across the front of their jersey.

There was no containing my excitement as I dashed back to my room. I had to call Mom and Dad! But I ended up hiding there for awhile as, from out in the hallway, I heard the reactions from some of the other players. Anger, disappointment and frustration dominated the discussions, as some players announced their intention to protest the results. I could understand their feelings; I knew how much this tryout had meant to all of us.

Finally, there was silence from the hallway. I opened the door a crack and the coast was clear. I ran quickly down the hall and out of the barracks. Determined to call my parents and share this moment with them, I crawled under the fence that surrounded the training center and spotted a pay phone at the 7-Eleven across the street.

When I heard Mom answer the phone I quickly blurted out, ''I made it!'' As happy as I was, I can't help but wonder if she was even more pleased. I could hear the pride in her voice when she quietly said, ''I knew you would.''

In the weeks before we left for the Pan-American Games, we traveled as a team to play against some very good competition around the country. A funny thing happened as I got ready to go to that first exhibition game, which was in Stratford, Connecticut. I got a notice about the game along with my plane ticket into fly to LaGuardia Airport. The notice told me that a limousine was going to pick me up from LaGuardia and bring me to Stratford.

I read that and I knew I had made the big time. Not only had my dream of playing for the United States come true, but I was being picked up in a limousine.

When I arrived at LaGuardia, I went looking for that long, black, stretch limousine that had picked me up so many times in my imagination. But it wasn't there. Instead, there was a blue van with orange lettering: Connecticut Limousine Service. Such is reality.

The Pan-American Games were played that year in Puerto Rico—most sports fans would remember it as the games when Indiana University Mens Basketball Coach Bobby Knight threw a chair across the court in an argument with a referee.

We went to San Juan and on the way over there we

heard that our team was the team that U.S. officials feared would be the target of terrorism. It was a heated time internationally. So we were guarded, as I am sure other teams were, by dozens of police officers.

But like most seventeen year-olds, terrorists weren't on my mind. Twix bars were. That was when the Twix bar first came out and they were given to us at the Pan-American Village cafeteria. We could have as many as we wanted. I had a Twix bar for every meal—and as a snack sometimes too.

When we lined up on the field for the first game, I became the youngest starter for the USA. I played second base and I hit second in our hitting rotation. We were winning our games pretty handily until we had our match against Belize.

Coach Raymond was so sure that we were going to beat Belize that he decided to start our second string. It got down to the seventh inning and we were behind 1-0. Coach decided it was time to send the starters in. He put me in as the leadoff batter and gave me the signal to lay down a bunt. He just wanted me to get on, then have the batters behind me get me around the bases.

I stood in the box and turned to face the pitcher. But as the ball came toward me, I pulled back. It was a strike. The next pitch came and I took a full swing, hit a ground ball and was thrown out. Coach Raymond asked me why I didn't lay down the bunt. I really didn't have an answer, but at the time, it just didn't feel right. That wasn't the answer he was looking for. He made a good point, and I learned a good lesson: When you're called on to do something, you have to do it with all your ability. And without hesitation.

I also learned a lesson that came from Coach Raymond's decision to play the second string until the end. It taught me that you can take no game for granted and that there are holes that even the best athletes can't dig out of.

The next two batters made quick outs and the USA had its only loss—at the hands of Belize.

Still, we entered the medal round of that tournament with a record of 9-1. It was the first time I had played under the international tournament rules, called the "Page System." In that system the top four teams from the tournament go to the medal round. Then number one plays number two. Number three plays number four. When three plays four it is a single elimination. The loser goes home, the winner jumps to a waiting position. When one plays two, it is like a double elimination. The loser of the one-two game goes to play the winner of three versus four. The winner of that game comes up to meet the winner of the one-two game for the gold medal—winner take all.

The deficiencies of the "Page System" were immediately apparent to me. We were to play Puerto Rico in the final game; a team we'd beaten twice already in the tournament. Yet if we lost to them in this final game, they'd win the gold.

Before the game, I remember having a calm lunch with two of my teammates, Kathy Strahan and Sue Enquist. I discussed the possibility of losing to Puerto Rico, and I will never forget the response I got from Kathy.

Matter of factly, she simply stated, "We are not going to lose." End of discussion.

I realized then that we must always have confidence in our teammates; it is believing that we are winners that produces the ability to win. If there is one ounce of doubt, it must be removed or we open the door to defeat.

A sense of calm came over me. Kathy's simple statement reaffirmed my belief in the team and our talents.

And just hours later, the United States had won the gold medal in the first ever Pan-American softball competition. To this day, that medal is among my most prized awards, as it was a great day for our sport and for our country.

It was about this time that I was introduced to the world of drug testing. I guess because I was always so hyper, they thought I was the perfect candidate for a drug test. I guess that's why I've been chosen in nearly every single tournament I've played. It's kind of embarrassing, actually. You're urinating in a cup and this woman is there watching to make sure it is actually your urine that you give them.

Two years later, I had the opportunity to wear those wonderful letters "USA" on my chest again.

The Orlando Rebels had won the National Championship in 1981, so we earned the right to represent our country as the national team in the 1982 World Championships in Taipei, Taiwan. It was the largest crowd I had ever played for. There were some 32,000 people in the stands. I was just turning twenty-one, and it was my first experience playing in front of that kind of crowd. In the Round Robin portion of the tournament, we went undefeated, 10-0, then we moved to the single elimination medal round.

In the bottom of the seventh inning of our first game, ahead two to one, a girl on the Taiwanese team crushed a home run ball that is still going today in left center. There was already a runner on first, so that homer beat us three to two. Among that unbelievable crowd in the stands, there might have been six Americans! The Taiwanese fans were jumping out of the stands, flags were waving, and they were going crazy.

That sent us into the loser's bracket game against Australia. We knew going in that the best that could happen was we would win the bronze. The worst was that we would finish fourth, something that had never happened to the U.S. team in the past.

Debbie Doom, a future UCLA Hall of Famer, was pitching for us. Australia's first batter hit a triple. Then the next pitch got by the catcher's glove, scoring the Australian player. We never even scored, losing one to zero. The United States finished fourth. No one could believe it.

There had never been, in my experience, a fourth place medal given in a tournament. That changed that year in Taiwan. When the Taiwanese realized that the United States finished fourth they went out and bought a medal for fourth place. It was an iron medal. They called us up on the stage and draped the iron medals around our necks in front of the rest of the world.

That iron medal was so heavy; I felt it trying to drag my head downward. In truth, I was hanging my head already. I accepted it with humility, but once I was back at the hotel, I stood in the stairways and wept. Disappointment and failure flowed from my eyes. Out of all the talented players our nation could boast, we'd been chosen to represent the United States. We hadn't just let ourselves down; we'd let down our country.

That tournament I was named to my first "All World" Team as shortstop. I had led all hitters with a .560 batting average. But these individual accomplishments were hollow, completely overshadowed by the fact that our team fell short of expectations. Individual glory is insignificant when compared to achieving victory as a team.

There have been times that I have played exceptionally well, been awarded numerous trophies, but the team had not played to its potential. Other times, I have performed marginally while the team has excelled. I would trade any individual award in exchange for a team victory.

The tears I had were not just because we lost. I had lost games many times before. The tears were so heavy because we represented our country. Whenever I have our country's uniform on, I feel I play for every softball player in the USA. I have No. 1 on my back, but not for Dot Richardson. No. 1 represents the pride I have in our country.

I have traveled all over the world. Since my name is Dorothy, I hear lots of jokes about the Wizard of Oz, and Toto, and Kansas, but there really is no place like home. When you travel to other countries, you know that it is a privilege and an honor to wear the uniform of the United States of America. I am so proud of the flag and all the lives that were given for that flag and our freedom. You feel it when you put that uniform on.

When we were in the Olympics, there were no individuals. I kept mentioning America in every interview. I was emphasizing that this is your team, I am your shortstop. It is as simple as that. I don't know why that patriotism might have been lost by other athletes, but for us in our sport, we know what it feels like not to get the opportunity to participate in the Olympics. So many of us could only dream about it, and only a few were able to achieve it. I felt that we achieved this for all of them.

In one interview after the Olympic Games, Candace Garvey brought up an interesting point when she said that so few of the athletes in the Olympics mentioned that they were doing it for the USA. She noted that most of them just emphasized their individual sacrifices. She said that she was proud of me because I had mentioned the USA so often.

I know I would love to be part of the 2000 Olympics in Sydney, and I will continue to work diligently, day by day, to achieve the goals I have set. For the past nine years I have been taking it year by year, each time pondering whether I'd be able to keep playing softball. Even working through my masters degree, medical school, and now my residency, I never knew if I would be able to play with all the commitment and responsibilities each year brings. Therefore, I still have to take it a year at a time and see where my goals and where my life lead me.

In the glory and excitement after the gold medal game, I told Byrant Gumbel in an interview that I would definitely try for the Sydney Olympics. But right after the interview, the backup shortstop came to me and said, ''Dot, you are not really going to try for 2000, are you?'' She said it in a way that really made me think. To any amateur or professional athlete, the Olympics is a dream. Would it be right for me to play again? I already have my medal. I understand her concern. I think for now I want to leave all options open. But if it becomes obvious to the coaches that the USA needs me, it would be hard not to answer the call.

CHAPTER

SIX

College

During high school, I realized that I would be able to use athletics to get a college education. I couldn't imagine a more exciting combination than receiving an education from one of the top institutions in the country while continuing to play the sports I loved.

One of the things that was so special about our Olympic team was how well-educated each player was. I wasn't alone in understanding the value of a diploma. We each knew, as women, that the greatest opportunity our talents in athletics could give us was an education. You see, having an education opens doors of opportunity, as well as, stimulating dreams. It is through schooling that we discover ourselves and the world around us. And in finding ourselves we creatively find ways our abilities can be used to make a contribution to society. The commitment each of us made to our education is one of those things that I wish had gotten more attention because I want young people to know the importance of using their talents to get ahead in life.

In many ways, female athletics today are where men were three decades ago. Think about the professional contracts signed by the male athletes only thirty years ago and compare them to those signed today. Ralph Raymond used to tell us how all the guys in the minor leagues would fight to drive the bus to their next game just to receive an extra dollar in their paycheck. Today we see the evolution of women's sports to the professional level. Yet, because there are still so few opportunities to make money from our athletic talents, we still have to be balanced, and take advantage of our educational opportunities. That's a message I try to share with everyone, but especially with young girls.

As I was coming out of high school, women's sports still were governed by the AIAW, the Association of Intercollegiate Athletics for Women. The NCAA, National Collegiate Athletic Association took over women's sports during my third year in college.

During my junior year in high school, UCLA won AIAW National Championships in four sports: volleyball, basketball, softball, and track. Those were the sports that I loved the most and to be able to attend a college where the top athletics were—well, I couldn't think of a more perfect dream. But it was definitely a dream. Could you imagine me, someone who lived on the opposite side of the country, who played slow-pitch softball in high school, and whose parents didn't want her going to school as far away as in California, at UCLA. No way was it going to happen! Besides, even the friends I told said it wasn't even possible.

Instead, I had a great opportunity to attend Western

Illinois University on a full-scholarship. It became possible when the coach Kathy Veroni, brought the team down to play against the Rebels for their spring training. When the coach saw some of the talent on our team she recruited those of us interested in college. At that time I was considering athletic training and attending Western was perfect since it was ranked tops in that field. Two of my teammates had been recruited by Western, and having friends there with me was also an advantage.

It was almost like the Rebels were a farm system for their team. Coach Veroni approached me during my junior year and asked if I would be interested in attending Western. I was flattered that she thought I was worthy of a scholarship and that I was considered good enough for her to want to coach. My parents were excited about this opportunity.

Many of the Florida colleges were also interested, but they played slow-pitch softball and my heart was in fast-pitch. However, there was another unexpected and tempting offer. It came from Texas A&M. Their coach flew out to see me. He explained that he was only able to come watch me play because he was visiting his brother. He said the Aggies wanted a lefty power hitter. I remember thinking that maybe he was mistaken about me. Yes, I could generate some power but I was known more for consistency. The more I thought about the offer the more serious I considered it. I read the brochures and the tradition was impressive. At the time, I was thinking about becoming a veterinarian; Texas A&M had one of the top programs in the country. It was also a bigger school. The only problem was I had verbally committed to Western and didn't want to disappoint the coach. I had given my word and they were counting on me. I felt I couldn't back out.

I remember the day I signed my letter of intent to Western Illinois. The one to Texas A&M was there beside it. While signing the letter to Western, I reminded Mom how I always dreamed of going to UCLA.

My freshman year at Western Illinois was fantastic. I competed in field hockey, a sport I had never even heard of before, as well as, basketball and softball. My mom remembers me calling at the start of the softball season to ask if she had ever heard of playing softball in a gymnasium. I did find it an excellent way to train however. Indoors allowed you to practice with fewer distractions.

That year we came in fifth in the nation in softball. I led the country with a .480 batting average and was nominated for the Broderick Award as the outstanding collegiate female athlete in the sport of softball. Everything was great on the field. Off the field, I majored in health and athletic training. And in many ways athletic training started my medical career. During my second semester, I volunteered with the school's physical therapist. As a result of that experience, I knew I wanted to continue in the health field to become a doctor.

One day I called Marge. She said Sharron Backus, the head coach at UCLA, called looking for players. Marge had commented to her that she was a year late; I had wanted to go to UCLA but was now attending Western. Marge suggested I call Coach Backus if I was still interested. When I talked to Coach Backus, I told her how much I dreamed about attending UCLA. I was shocked when she said they were interested in me, too. She said that if I really wanted to transfer to UCLA I should make my decision soon because in a couple of years colleges will be joining the NCAA. That would mean I would have to sit out, while if I transferred soon, under the AIAW rules I wouldn't have to. I couldn't believe what I was hearing. I could get to UCLA. But then I woke up! I would be letting everyone down especially Coach Veroni. Besides, I didn't think my parents would let me!

The only solution was to complete two years at Western and then transfer to UCLA—even knowing I would have to sit out a year. It was really hard when I told Kathy Veroni what I was thinking of doing. In fact it was so difficult because I knew I had disappointed her. She told me I couldn't leave because she had recruited the next class off me. After some soul searching, I decided to stay at Western. Everything would be okay. I would let down less people if I stayed. I just wouldn't live this particular dream.

Then the phone rang. It was my big sister, Kathy. She said, ''Look, Mom and Dad aren't going to tell you what to do, but I am. You are going to go to UCLA. It is the best thing for you. You have never done a selfish thing in your life, but you are going to do it now. You are going to UCLA.'' I told her that I didn't think that I could, that I would love to go but everyone at Western would be so disappointed in me. She insisted that it was the right move for me. I can still feel all the indecision, the distress, the tears. But I followed my sister's advice and made the decision to live my dream.

Not only did I leave an institution that had treated me great, but one where I was allowed to play three sports and compete as the shortstop, my favorite position in my favorite sport. In the discussion with UCLA, I was told I was needed as the second baseman. I hesitated at the thought but felt being at UCLA was worth the change. In the back of my mind, I hoped when Coach Backus saw me play for the first time she would know I was a shortstop. At UCLA, they already had a good shortstop, Patti Irving.

Once I got to UCLA, I tried out for the varsity basketball team along with softball. I was called into the office and told I couldn't play for the varsity basketball team because the season would overlap that of softball. However, I could play junior varsity basketball because the season was shorter and ended before softball started. Since softball was paying for my education, my first obligation was to it.

My parents and grandparents drove me out to Los Angeles. It was on my 19th birthday. After they had left, Coach Backus asked me to go to the softball field. When I arrived, I was surprised to see a field totally hidden among the trees. It had only two small bleachers. WOW! Some change from the facility of today! At the field Coach Backus and three Bruin players, Nedra Jerry, Frankie Butler, and Patti Irving were painting bleachers.

After the introductions, Coach Backus said, ''Dot and Patti get at shortstop and let me hit you some ground balls.'' Patti was first, then me. We each had three balls hit to us. Then she told Patti to move over to second.

I didn't realize it at the time but that was my tryout. I was the shortstop. Patti ended up leaving the team later in the season. I felt bad about that and went to talk to Coach. I remember telling her that if Patti was leaving because she wanted to be at shortstop I would gladly move to second. The team would be stronger with her in the line-up. Coach said "No, I have made my decision." Later I found out from teammates, that when they heard I was coming, they were excited.

I went down the next day to coach's office and sat across the desk from her. "You don't remember me, do you?" She asked what I meant. I told her I had played with the Orlando Rebels against her in Stratford, Connecticut in 1975. She couldn't believe it. She asked how old I had been, and I told her I was thirteen. She smiled and said, "You were the little kid in right field!" I reminded her about the incredible feat I had accomplished by getting a base hit off the pitching legend Joan Joyce, and also how I admired her style of play.

While at UCLA, we went to the nationals all three years—once under the AIAW, twice with the NCAA. Not too many people know this, but each of my last "at bats" in the collegiate national championships I was intentionally walked. I bring it up because I learned a valuable lesson that I carry with me both on and off the field. When you think of an intentional walk, as a hitter you think it's "cool" because it shows the other team is afraid of your abilities. I guess you could look at it as a form of respect. But when you're standing on first base thinking these thoughts, you realize an opportunity has passed. Then, it hits you, "It is better to try and fail than to never have the opportunity to try."

My junior year at UCLA, 1982, the first ever NCAA Championships were held. We played against Fresno State and won, and UCLA captured the NCAA Softball Championship. ESPN was there covering the game with one camera. I was especially excited about winning because the seniors that worked so hard for so long went out as national champs.

The next year we were determined to go out on top, and nothing was going to stop us. We had a great team with players like Sheila Cornell, who later became the first baseman on the Olympic team. We were awesome! We were ranked number one throughout the season and went to Omaha, Nebraska for the NCAA Championships.

Our first game was against Louisiana Tech. The stands were packed. We won seven–to–zero. I went four–for–four, Sheila Cornell had a grand-slam home run. The team was hot! When we left the field everyone knew who was going to win the tournament. In fact, the biggest question was who was going to come in second. That was how dominating we were. We all went out to eat dinner after the game, nothing unusual. A number of us ordered milkshakes. I recall mine didn't taste all that great.

The next morning I woke up early. I didn't feel very well. I rushed to the bathroom and got sick. I went to lay down but I couldn't go back to sleep. There was a knock on my hotel room door. It was my teammates asking if I wanted to go eat breakfast. I told them that I didn't feel well. They immediately said ''Ugh, everybody's got it!'' Eight out of nine starters had food poisoning. Each of us grabbed a small trash can from the hotel rooms and took it to the game. To this day everyone calls us the 'bucket brigade.'' You know in your life when you take certain mental pictures? Well, one of mine is when the team walked in to the stadium and some of the guys at the top of the bleachers looked down and asked, "What are the buckets for?" And I said, "Well, you'll see in a minute." We had the whole routine down: if somebody got sick, there would be one person to hold the hair back, one person would have a cold towel to compress on the back of the neck, one person would be holding the bucket. It was disgusting, but we had a national tournament game to play.

We were playing Fullerton. I was leadoff batter and got a double. As I stood on second base, I started feeling worse. I called time out. The athletic trainer came running out with my bucket, and I got sick. I felt awful but we had a game to win. The next girl came up to bat and got a hit. I rounded third, was waved home and scored.

To this day you can look at the newspaper article about that game and see that I collapsed into the arms of the on-deck batter, Barbara Booth. You can see my face, and I am as white as a sheet. I had no energy.

We were up one to zero. But, Fullerton started hitting the ball and scored four runs in the fourth inning. Finally, Coach said, 'That's it.' She took the worst of us, Tracy Compton, Sue Eskerski, and myself out of the game and sent us back to the hotel to see a doctor. We were given medicine and told to lie down. Shortly after, I got a call from our assistant coach, Sue Enquist. She asked how I was feeling and could I play. I asked if we had won. We had lost six to one. It was a double elimination tournament so even with that loss we were still in the running. I said, "I'm there. I know I can play. It's the national champion-ship!"

The three of us were brought to the field and the whole team ran over to the right field fence to greet us. We were to play the University of South Carolina. Darlene Lowery who later made the next Pan-American Team was pitching against us. We went 21-innings—and WON! The score was two to one. At that time there was no international tie breaker rule. By winning, we got to play another day. I remember saying "Thank you, Lord for helping us make it."

If you have ever had food poisoning, you know that the next day you are still very weak. But our next game was against Texas A&M. They had some key players in their shortstop Carrie Austin and pitcher Lori Stoll. She was a left-handed pitcher with a really strong arm. She could gun the ball.

We were down by one run in the bottom of the seventh inning. I was up to bat with the tying run on second and two outs. They walked me. Our next batter hit a grounder to short for the third and final out of the game. We lost. That year, we did not go out as national champions, we came in third.

It wasn't until my senior year at UCLA that I learned what it meant to be a "true champion." It's not winning the game that makes you a champion. I learned it's not being at least one run ahead of the other team, either. I have never played on another team that I have been more proud of. Because we never gave up, we never made excuses, we gave everything we had! It may not have been our best performance but it was the best that we could give under the circumstances. That's what it means to be a champion—to give everything you have in all that you do. Maybe not all of us will one day be able to say "I am an All-American, a state, or national champion, or even

Focused from the beginning.

Little brother Lonnie and me.

Brother Kenny's baseball team, Brother Lonnie is the best bat
boy. . . . Bat girl not in picture . . . me!

Seventh grade.

Me at 10 years old and my first softball team!

It's not the trophies
or the medals. . . .
It's living your
dreams.

Big Sky and riding high at my sister Kathy's home in Montana.

1979 USA Pan American Team, San Juan, Puerto Rico.

Mom and me.

College years with Sue Enquist and Sue Eskierski.

1981 World Championship in Tokyo, Japan.

Kinesiology Graduation from UCLA with Suzie Stokes.

Pre-Olympic billboard: Welcome to Orlando.

Media Day.

US Olympic Festival in Denver,
Colorado carrying the flame
of HOPE.

USA Shortstop.

Support a teammate . . . stand your ground. *(AP/Wide World Photo/Joe Cavaretta)*

Turning it. *(AP/Wide World Photo/Eric Drotter)*

The Dream Team!

WE DID IT AMERICA! *(AP/Wide World Photo/Elise Amendola)*

All of the family
and the Gold.

Living the dream for everyone. . . . Sharing the Gold! *(AP/Wide World Photo/Nick Ut)*

Throwing out the first pitch at the 1996 World Series in Atlanta, New York Yankees vs. Atlanta Braves.

Tom and me. . . . He's always been there for me
and together we are making a difference.

Dave and me before going out into the streets of New York to hit
some balls. *(AP/Wide World Photo/Alan Singer)*

UCLA Hall of Fame Induction.

My post-Olympic surprise birthday party. I'd never celebrated a birthday with 500 people before.

At our church, Faith Methodist.

Everyone's motivated. It's fun to share my love of the game.

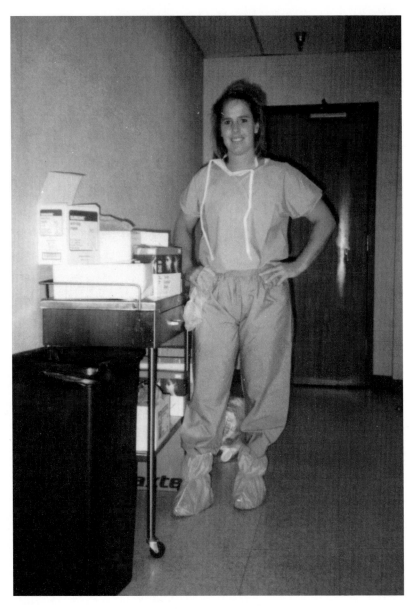

Ready for surgery.

an Olympic Gold Medalist,'' but all of us will be able to say we are ''true champions'' if we have worked hard to be the best we can be.

During my years at UCLA, I had led the team in hitting each year and later was named the NCAA's Player of The Decade for the 1980s. After I graduated, a number of people were encouraging me to make a run at playing major league baseball. Even Coach Backus thought I could make it.

Remember UCLA is the school that produced Anne Myers, who was a good enough basketball player that she got a tryout in the NBA. Though Anne didn't make it, she earned a lot of respect for women basketball players by giving it a try. I think that's what some women wanted from me in baseball.

But I was more excited about the possibilities developing with softball. I know it may sound funny that when I was younger all I wanted was to play baseball, and then at 22 years of age I wasn't interested anymore. It's because I found fast-pitch softball.

CHAPTER

SEVEN

Allyson

A benefit of playing with one of the best teams in the country, like the Orlando Rebels, is the opportunity to play against great competition. And for me, being able to play in front of my family was an added bonus. From the moment I first saw the Raybestos Brakettes, I knew that to wear their uniform would be like playing for the New York Yankees. The team was full of tradition and included many of the legends of the sport. Even as a bat girl, I could feel they were champions. I felt that once I played on that team it was a sign that I was making my mark in softball.

The first time that the admiration became mutual was when I was sixteen and the Rebels played a game in Allentown, Pennsylvania. Brakette Coach Ralph Raymond watched me play there and I guess he liked what he saw. It was only my second year at shortstop, but people were saying I could be good at the position. Ralph agreed.

I went on to play that year for Coach Raymond at the Pan-American Games and afterwards, he asked me if I'd consider being a Brakette. What a tribute! I said no at the time because my family lived in Orlando, but he let me know that whenever I wanted, the door was open.

In 1984, after nine years with the Rebels, I decided to take coach Raymond up on his offer. I became a Brakette.

The excitement of becoming a Brakette was to be able to play with the best players in the sport, including their incredible second baseman, Allyson Rioux. I'll never forget the first time I met Ally; it was the previous year, at the end of the National Championships while I was still with the Rebels. There was a knock on my hotel room door, and when I opened it there was a woman with the friendliest eyes and the warmest smile. We had never met before, only knowing of each other through competition. Now she was standing at my door telling me how excited she was that we would be teammates next season. She also quietly whispered, as if to let me in on a big secret, ''we are going to be the best middle infield combination the sport has ever known.'' Then from behind her back, she pulled a T-shirt with the Raybestos logo on the front and ''Richardson,'' along with the number one, across the back.

Not only was Allyson a good friend and an incredible player, she was a great person. She was a big part of the reason I became a Brakette. She was always willing to give of herself for her team, and everyone respected her for it. It wasn't until after I joined the team, for example, that I learned she had given up her jersey number one so that Ralph could offer it to me when I joined the team. It was a little thing, but it told me she wanted me there. And it was an example of how she always put others needs above hers.

That's the type of person she was. She was very giving and caring, a strong Christian and very home-oriented. She believed in family and she did everything in her power to make others feel important. Her father died when she was younger, but before he died, he instilled in her a love for baseball. She loved the game, but she loved people even more. And everyone returned her love because she always thought about others long before herself.

Allyson became my roommate while on the road. We shared a lot of laughs, many tears and dreams together. She was one of the greatest defensive players ever to put on a glove. She had incredible hands, so sure that her nickname was "Hoover," for the vacuum cleaner. For six years, we were teammates, roommates, and above all, friends. We built the reputation, and over and over again demonstrated we were one of the best double combos the sport had ever assembled.

It was the summer of 1986 when the team found out that Allyson was sick. She had been diagnosed with a brain tumor. When I first saw her that season, she came to watch a game and was sitting in the stands wearing a yellow sundress with a large hat. She took the hat off during the game and showed her bald head. Allyson always had thick black hair, but the radiation treatments caused her hair to fall out. She was so alive and energized. It seemed nothing ever got her down. She was so proud of us and told us she would be back in uniform by nationals. It was true.

She came back for nationals—which was an inspiration to the team and to everyone that knew her. She wore a baseball helmet to protect her head. We were protective of her at first until we quickly realized she needed no protection. Her style of play had never changed. She said that was only a taste of things to come; she was returning the following season and no one would know she had dealt with these troubles. Allyson was on her way to recovery.

At the beginning of the season, Allyson was looking better than I had ever seen her. I will never forget the first road trip when she came into the room and told me, "I know I have a brain tumor, but it's not going to hold us back. We are going to show the world what we can do by capturing the National Championship." I understood what she was telling me. In her own way she was telling me she didn't want it to be an issue. That she was ready to move forward. She was prepared to play and competing made it easier to cope with her illness.

We both went on to have phenomenal years. We went to nationals and she was fantastic. She made All-American. She was hitting, playing great defense and, as Allyson hoped, we won the national championship!

After nationals, Allyson was named the head softball coach at Sacred Heart University in Bridgeport, Connecticut—her dream coaching job. She was so happy. She was able to work at a competitive softball program that was close to her home, was an all-American, and a national champion.

It was February 9, 1989. I was in my first year of medical school and was preparing for an examination for the following Monday when I got a phone call. It was Pat Dufficy, one of our teammates. She was crying when she told me. Allyson had passed away that morning. I was in shock. I had no idea that her headaches had started recurring. I couldn't say a word for the longest time.

A short time later, I called her cousin, Bobby Sabia, who told me what had happened. Allyson started her coaching job and everything seemed great until Bobby started to notice that Allyson was falling asleep during the day while sitting at her desk. Almost every time he came to her office to visit she was sleeping. He knew something was wrong, and insisted she go to the doctors. He told me he was worried she would fall asleep while driving home. That's how bad it had gotten.

She was in a hospital in New York City and all the best neurosurgeons tried to see what they could do. They determined it was inoperable. Since she already had gotten the maximum dosage of radiation, Allyson was brought home from the hospital to be with her family in the last days of her life. I know that is where she would have wanted to be.

I flew to Connecticut for her funeral. It was the most moving experience in my life. I think one of the hardest things to deal with is death, especially when it comes to someone so young. She died when she was twenty-seven. I remember it was a very cold and dreary day. It was winter in February in New England and the ground was still hard from the cold. At the wake I saw her family for the first time since the last season. Her mom was seated. When I saw Mrs. Rioux, I couldn't help myself. The energy that held me up had left my legs and I fell to my knees. We embraced and I couldn't stop crying. ''Allyson loved playing next to you,'' her mom said as we held each other. ''She was always so proud of that. It's just time now for her to spend time with her father. Her father has missed her,'' she said. When you meet her mom, you can see where Allyson found her strength.

People had flown in from all over the world to be there in her memory. Every Brakette was there. Allyson's mom appointed eight of us to be her honorary pallbearers. We walked in front of the casket and Allyson was carried to the front of the church. They were the hardest and loneliest steps I've ever taken.

It was such a beautiful church. In fact, I was told it was Allyson's favorite. She would go there every Sunday she was home. Allyson rarely missed church. God gave her strength. Even on the road, she and Ralph would go together to a nearby Catholic church. A very young preacher, one of Allyson's favorites, presided. I remember her talking about him all the time. That day he was talking about her. He said the most beautiful words—for the most beautiful of people. I will always remember her mom as she collapsed over the casket to hug her daughter one more time. They were the best of friends. If there was one person in this world that Allyson would want to be like, it was her mom. She loved her with all her heart.

During the ceremony, I realized that this was the first time Ally was to my right. I missed her so much already. When the procession of cars followed the hearse, I was positioned in the middle, and when I looked back there were miles of cars. I thought, ''Allyson, look at all who love you. Look at all the lives you have touched. Your life meant so much to so many people. This is how you deserve to go out.'' Maybe it's true. The good do die young.

Allyson was buried in her red Brakette uniform. Her family knew how much the team meant to her.

I have to say that through all the sadness I saw the beauty of sport. That through sports and caring for people, someone can make a difference in the lives of others. You meet hundreds, thousands of people, and if you choose, you can help shape some of their lives. There were people there that didn't know Allyson for long but when they had met her, they were moved by her. They will never forget her. It was through her life in sports that Allyson grew into an inspiring person—the perfect example of how sports can help develop you as a person.

Allyson Rioux left me with the lesson to keep life in perspective and to remember how truly mortal we all are. She lived her life to the fullest, constantly placing other people's needs ahead of her own. Though it has been over eight years since her death, not a day goes by that I don't think about her, especially during softball season. As I stood on the Olympic gold medal podium in Columbus, I thought about Ally and the role she'd played in guiding our sport to this finest of moments. I know she was there with us, and I know she was proud.

She was such a gift from God.

EIGHT

Becoming "Doctor Dot"

Loving athletics as much as I do, you can imagine that I had more than my share of injuries while growing up. As a result, I got a first-hand look at what being a doctor was all about. Or so I thought.

It's ironic that I chose to become a doctor, given that I hated hospitals as a child. Perhaps it started at birth. My mom said the umbilical cord was wrapped around my neck and I was blue when I was born! The earliest recollection I have of my distaste for medicine was when I was five years old. We had just moved to England where my dad was stationed in the Air Force. There was no housing available so we lived off the base in Peasonhall. I remember playing with lots of the neighborhood kids.

One day we were all taking turns sliding down a wooden slide. I put my hands along the outside edges of the slide and on the way down a sliver of wood embedded into my right ring finger. The pain was excruciating, but I didn't want to tell my parents because I'd been warned that I could get hurt doing it. In typical five-year-old fashion, I guess I didn't want to prove them right.

I finally told my parents a few hours later. They brought me to the hospital and even the doctors couldn't get it out without surgery. They put me in this big room where all my roommates were boys, with injuries more "glamorous" than mine. A couple of them were in traction with their broken legs hanging up in the air.

The next morning I was taken to the operating room. They put this plastic mask over my face and I thought I was going to suffocate, but then I started to see colorful lines circling around and around and around . . . next thing I knew, I was within a plastic tent and slowly my eyes focused on a figure in the distance. When the clouds cleared, there was my mom. I was scared to be in the plastic "thing." What had happened? What was wrong? Then I was told that while they were removing the splinter, half of my lung had collapsed and I was put in the oxygen tent. Not an ideal first visit to a hospital.

When I was younger, choosing a career in medicine would have been one of my last choices. I look back at those experiences now and realize I was scared by just the thought of seeing a physician. Like most patients, it was because I didn't understand what was going on. I always thought of them as little more than the bearers of bad news and big needles. It was all a mystery. They never seemed to explain what was happening in a way I could understand.

It wasn't until the tenth grade, during a biology class, that my understanding of medicine started to change. We dissected a cat and I was fascinated by the anatomy and how everything in the body worked. I didn't tell anyone at the time, but that was when I first started to think about becoming a doctor.

Athletics without a doubt had prepared me for my career in medicine. There are so many similarities between the two, it's amazing: the opportunity to meet and appreciate other people, the physical skills of coordination and dexterity, as well as the mental challenges of concentration, determination, and dedication. In athletics, you learn to set goals to improve yourself so you can give more to the team. You develop a drive to give everything you have no matter what the circumstances. But the stakes are higher in medicine; the difference is not in the outcome of a game, but in the lives of other people.

With all the similarities, there is a very significant difference between softball and medicine, and that is in the definition of success. In softball, three hits out of ten at-bats is considered great!!! As a surgeon, a .300 average is not even considered adequate; in fact, you won't even make the team.

It is truly a blessing to have learned lessons and developed skills on the athletic field that helped me become a better surgeon. Mostly, athletics taught me how to work well with other people, and to appreciate their individual talents. Such qualities are as necessary for doctors as they are for athletes.

A surgeon has to know how to work together with others as a team in order to perform a successful surgery. A surgeon does not work alone. From the moment you walk into the operating room, there is an anesthesiologist, a scrub tech, a scrub nurse, and a number of other supportive personnel. They're all there to help make the surgery go smoothly. It is the team's effort that makes a difference in the outcome.

Combining softball with medicine has certainly been a challenge. I have to take each day at a time. I plan my athletics around my hospital responsibilities, because in order to play, I need to make sure my doctor's schedule is clear. I have missed many games and tournaments because of duties in the hospital. But I have been fortunate because I have been on softball teams that have supported me one hundred percent. They knew that with my schedule, I would miss practices and games. There have been times when I have flown from medical school in Louisville, Kentucky or from my residency program at LAC-USC in Los Angeles, California across country to be able to play with the Raybestos Brakettes.

On arrival, I would be picked up by my old stand by Connecticut Limousine Service and driven to Bridgeport, where a van would be there to pick me up. I would change into my uniform while we were driving to the field, or change in the locker room as soon as I got there. As soon as I got to the stadium, I would put on my cleats and start warming-up. Then I'd tell Coach Raymond that I was ready, and he would immediately put me into the game at shortstop. By this time, it was usually the second inning of the second game of the doubleheader.

I would play in the Saturday and Sunday doubleheaders and then take the limousine service to LaGuardia Airport and fly back. The first month of my residence program overlapped with my softball season, so this routine was from coast-to-coast. At this point, I realized the situation was simply too demanding and had to come to an end. It so happened that Ralph Raymond announced his retirement at the end of that season, so my decision to transfer to a local team in southern California was much easier to make.

My two careers have often conflcited and battled for my attention, causing a lot of tough times and a lot of heartaches. Yes, I've been blessed with a lot of accomplishments, but each one has taken hard work and dedication. There have been many victories, but also some serious sacrifices as I worked to find the right balance between medical school and softball.

My first major defeat came when I was in my second year of medical school in 1990. At the year's end, I took the boards that would allow me to go on to the next year of school. Throughout that year, I had done what was required at school but in the upcoming months before the exam my focus was on the excitement of making the USA World Championship team. I had thought it would be my third and last World Championship. I was amazed that I even had the chance to tryout, and I was determined to make the best of it. I would go to the batting cage and fine tune my swing, work on ground balls, and tirelessly strengthen my throwing arm.

The board exam was scheduled a couple of weeks after our academic year was completed. I crammed for the exam, but made sure my softball practice time didn't suffer. I left for the Olympic Training Center after I finished taking the two day examination. At the end of the tryout, I was named to the USA World Championship team! It worked out perfectly because the World Championships were the last week of my vacation month. I took the examination seriously—with two years of medical school behind me I thought I had prepared enough. But I was wrong.

A classmate and my best friend at medical school, Walter Montgomery, drove up to see me play at the World Championships held in Normal, Illinois only a five hour drive from Louisville. He brought with him the results of my exam. I struggled to accept what he was telling me. "You've got to be kidding me, I failed the test?" I didn't comprehend failure, especially in academics. In my mind, I went over how I had prepared for the exam. Over and over again, I came up with the conclusion that I needed to put more effort into my studies. I needed to develop a stronger commitment than the one I was giving.

I was given the choice of retaking the exam, or repeating the entire year. I elected to repeat my second year then retake the test. I felt I needed to devote myself more to my commitment of becoming a great doctor.

My personal life has also been a victim of my drive to succeed in two careers. Walter was a great friend, and though I wasn't completely aware of it at the time, softball and medicine demanded that I sacrifice any chance of a relationship with him. We had met during our interview at the University of Louisville Medical School. I fell in love with him the first time I saw him. He was tall with dark hair, with a kind and warm personality. We became very close, and I was confused at times as to whether we were dating or just best of friends. I missed him whenever I was away playing softball, but found it difficult to express all that I felt for him.

Often, he would travel to watch me play, and then brag

to everyone in medical school of my prowess on the field. I could tell he was proud of me. He was one of the few men I had met who overtly showed other people how proud he was of me and my athletic abilities, without ever being intimidated by it. There were some memorable evenings when we would play catch in the parking lot next to the library, underneath the lights. There was no comparisons or competition between us in sport. There was no ego that got in the way.

Since I had elected to repeat a year, Walter was now a year ahead of me. I was devoted to doing the best I could, which meant turning down invitations to parties, camping, or movies. I was not going to let myself down again, so my commitment to medicine had to equal my commitment to athletics. I started working even harder and did very well, honoring a lot of my classes and rotations. But it had a price.

Walter moved on to someone who had more time for him. He met a nurse and they started dating. Last I heard they were together and considering marriage. I thought he would always be there. I was wrong. I took him for granted so many times. At first I tried to fight for him when I heard he was in love with this nurse, but it was too late. Finally I realized that he deserved somebody who had more time for him, even though I had imagined we would be together after medical school. Sadly, I never let him know how very special he was to me.

After repeating that year of school, it was time to repeat the exam. Afterwards, I flew to the Olympic Training Center to tryout for the USA Pan-American Team. The need to try and represent our country is a dream that always burns brightly. It was my vacation month and I felt I had to try again, but this time I had not touched a ball since the national tournament held nine months before.

I was hoping to make history by becoming the only player to be named to four consecutive U.S. Pan-American softball teams. The tryouts began the next day and lasted a week. It was the longest week of my life. I wasn't prepared to tackle either the demands of the rigid schedule or the pitches of our nation's premiere shooters, and it showed. I had my moments but they were few and far between. At the end of the week they posted the final team roster in the dorm.

Silently, I walked down the dormitory hallway to see if I had made it. People stood in their doorways as I headed toward the postings. I knew, and the list confirmed this, that I was not named to the Pan-American Team. In my mind, I had failed. Most of the players who were not named to the team left the training center bright and early the next morning. I decided to stay and support my friends and teammates who'd be representing the USA, though I was very humbled by the looks everyone gave me.

One of the toughest things I had to swallow was knowing that I was not selected as one of the two coaches selection. I knew I had not earned the position of shortstop by my performance at the tryouts but I felt not being chosen as a coach's selection was a disappointment.

It was hard to accept. Initially, I was of the opinion that if the coach believed I could make a difference to the team, then I should have been selected. She knew what I was capable of doing. I had competed against her team many times, and she was aware of my experience level and my recent athletic accomplishments. Ultimately, I was more disappointed in myself because I did not prepare properly. I had hoped my reputation would carry me through the tryouts. I reminded myself that more time had been needed to study for the boards, and that I'd been willing to face the consequences. I just didn't know how painful they could be.

I realized I couldn't keep doing both—that something was going to have to give. Not making that team sent the message that it might be time to hang up my glove and cleats. But it was an old saying that restored much of my faith, and encouraged me to persevere. "One who fails to prepare, prepares to fail."

I made up my mind to continue to do my best at both medicine and softball. I just wasn't ready to give up on either one. I had learned great lessons from these failures: I had to keep my priorities straight, and that I was naive to hope that I could live off my reputation. Now I was going to put all my education to work on both the softball diamond and the operating table.

Those nights of studying did pay dividends, though. Not only did I pick up my grades and pass the boards, but I went on to honors in nearly every subject. My commitment and my understanding that my medical degree was going to get me a top-flight position as a resident had made me a success in the classroom. There was a real satisfaction in knowing that I was more than a successful athlete; I was also a successful student.

During my fourth year of medical school I began the process of trying to get into an orthopedic surgery residency program. I had passed my boards, and I had interviewed at some great universities throughout the country. Now I had to wait to see where I would "match." Each fourth year medical student makes a list that shows the order of residency programs they prefer to attend. Then the residency programs ranks all the fourth-year medical students that they invited to interview at their institutions. The lists are put into a computer which "matches" the rank lists. By sheer chance, the day I turned in my match list was the day I learned that softball had been announced as a medal sport in the 1996 Olympics.

My dual careers were to collide once again, and it seemed as though I might finally have to make the decision that firmly put either medicine or softball at the top of my priorities. Two questions kept running through my mind. First, would I even match? And second, would I match at a program which would support my dream of competing in the Olympics?

CHAPTER

NINE

Countdown

Though I was tremendously excited when it was announced in 1993 that softball was to become a medal sport in the upcoming '96 Olympics, I was still waiting to see where I would be doing my residency. And of course, there was the definite possibility that the resident program wouldn't be very supportive of my Olympic aspirations. Would they understand that I was absolutely committed to representing the United States in Atlanta?

Nevertheless, I was soon informed that I had been matched at the Los Angeles County/University of Southern California Medical Center. At first, I was not terribly vocal about my Olympic dream, as I hoped to advance deep into the tryouts without needing to ask my new bosses at the hospital for time off.

The way the tryouts were set up, they allowed just about anyone to attend the Level One camps, with the best players being invited to Level Two camps. Then the top sixty from Level Two would gather in Oklahoma City to join a pre-invited sixty athletes for the third and final level. The pre-selected sixty players were All-Americans at both the collegiate and national levels.

As I had been named an Amateur Softball Association All-American the year before, I was able to skip straight to the Level Three camp. That was extremely important to me, because I didn't have extra weekends off from work to go climb through the first two levels.

Following the 1995 Pan-American games, in which the U.S. won the gold medal, all the players' conversations focused around making the Olympic squad. Such was the dedication among these women that many had quit their jobs or moved back in with their parents because they had no source of financial income. People had put themselves on training schedules with personal trainers.

I had to wonder if my residency, and the time it required, would hinder my chances when it came time to tryout against these women who had dedicated themselves to making the team. I knew, having failed to make the Pan-American team a few years earlier, that reputations would mean nothing when it came to selecting fifteen Olympians from millions of softball players. The Olympics were important to me, but so was being an orthopedic surgeon. I did not want to lose my residency position, nor did I want to not try my best at making the team. So I had to make some adjustments.

To keep in shape, I purchased a tread mill and lifted weights 2-3 times a week. Also, I put a large net in my bedroom so I could practice hitting balls in the evenings after work. I would set up a batting tee and a soft-toss machine and work on my swing. The bedroom in my apartment was quite big, so I just placed the hitting net at the base of the bed. It was perfect.

One morning when I left for work, there was a letter on my front door. The letter requested that I kindly train for the Olympics at a more reasonable hour. Remembering that I'd been jogging away on the treadmill late the night before, I felt badly about being inconsiderate. But I had to smile, because I wondered if my neighbor truly knew that's what I was training for.

It was March, 1995 when my boss, Dr. Patzakis, called me into his office. He is the Chairman of Orthopedic Surgery at LAC/USC, and my surprise was complete when he informed me that the board had decided to give me a year leave of absence from the hospital to train for the Olympic squad. I had no idea that they were even entertaining the possibility that I'd make the team. *I* wasn't even sure that I was going to make it!

So after finishing my second year of residency, I hung up my doctor's scrubs and focused on the final summer of trying out. On July 1st I reported to Denver, Colorado for the Olympic Festival.

The tension was high and the competition stiff, but perhaps most memorable was the excitement of all the participants. For myself it was a wonderful time, as I swelled with the pride and patriotism of being selected by my fellow athletes to carry the torch in the opening ceremonies. I was notified early in the day and brought over to Mile High Stadium to practice the run up the many, many steps.

That night during the opening ceremonies I got the first true taste of what the Olympics might be like. The stadium was crammed to capacity as I sat in the Denver Broncos locker room, watching from a television all the festivities and waiting for my cue to get onto the field and seize the torch. Hearing the noise and enthusiasm from the crowd only heightened the anticipation, and I was reminded of the honor my peers had bestowed upon me.

My cue arrived and I was directed onto the field. As I came from around the corner of the stage, I was overwhelmed by the immensity of the crowd. The torch was handed off to me after it had made it around the infield. At this time the announcement was made as to who was carrying the torch, as it had been kept secret from both the public and the athletes. My fellow softball players were stunned as they realized that I was carrying that torch not only for the United States, but for our sport as well. We had finally reached a new level of respect and recognition.

When I stopped at the bottom of the steps and presented the torch up high for all to see, the crowd erupted into thunderous applause. Climbing those steps was an appropriate symbol for the new heights that softball had reached.

The next day we started the competition. It was at this point that I sustained an injury on what seemed to be a routine play. I swung on a Lisa Fernandez outside pitch and felt a minor twinge in my neck. The ball went foul. I hit the next ball and as I ran to first the pain in my neck was excruciating. It felt as if I had hyperextended my neck.

As the game wore on, I started having spasms, to the point where I couldn't move my neck. This tournament was so important to my making the team that I continued to play, despite the pain. The next time up to bat, it was so bad I had to turn and face the pitcher instead of standing sideways, as you would normally. I had to face her in order to try to hit. Playing in the field, I couldn't even look to first base when I threw the ball. I just aimed on instinct and feeling.

The coaches didn't have me play the next game and had a chiropractor working on my neck. It felt temporarily good enough that I could play the following game, hoping to continue to impress the Olympic coaches.

Big mistake. During that game, I dove for a ball, and I hyperextended my neck again. It just kept getting worse. Against my instincts, I kept playing, but I just tried to take it easy.

I sat out one day. I had to get back onto the field. This was it. There was no tomorrow. It was amazing how the tryout process was changing each of us. It changed a team sport into an individual sport.

I remember going for a ball up the middle and wondering if I should have caught it. Could another shortstop have gotten it? Did the selection committee think I should have gotten it? It was emotionally and physically demanding, but above all it started each of us thinking more about our own performances as opposed to the overall play of the team. We were finding ourselves thinking of little else but our own efforts. That was the part I hated, and it didn't really hit me till the end of the process.

Ralph Raymond was announced as the head coach for the Olympic Team. It was a historic moment. He deserved the honor for all his dedication to both the sport and to us players. He couldn't keep the tears from flowing. It showed how much he wanted it. The selection committee named the two assistant coaches, Margie Wright and Ralph Weekly.

As the final tryouts approached, the pressure began to build. You could see it in everyone's eyes. I can't count the times the players would talk about who should be chosen. It was getting to the point where everyone just wanted the process over.

That summer, I was asked by a newspaper what I thought the feeling would be for the players chosen to the first ever USA Olympic softball team. After a moment's consideration, I replied that for about a minute they will be on top of the clouds, and then they will feel the lowest when they remembered those who would be left behind.

The final tryout. I actually felt it was more of a celebration. Once more, the top players in the country were brought together for the final time. It was so impressive to see the talent. It was great to see the youngsters gaining experience, so that they might represent us in the future.

Even though I continued to be immensely affected by my neck injury, my last at-bat during a tryout game was a home run over the center field fence. I didn't know then what the future held, but as I rounded the bases I thanked God for allowing me the opportunity to compete.

After that last tryout game, the committee adjourned to select the final fifteen players and the five alternates. We were informed that the list would be handed out in the hospitality room at the hotel at seven the next morning. Then at seven-thirty the team and the alternates would meet in a room together to prepare for a press conference. In the meantime all those that were not on the list were to pack and fly home.

It's hard to describe the conflicting senses of relief and anxiety we all felt. Many of us went to dinner to attempt to unwind; it didn't work. Nothing could keep our mind from the thought of seven o'clock that following morning. I couldn't sleep. To keep occupied, I decided to get everybody's autograph who was at the tryout. Of course I didn't get everyone, but it killed time until about four in the morning.

I headed back to my room. Christa Williams, one of the young pitchers at seventeen years of age, was in the room playing *Scrabble®* with Lisa. We talked for a while, then I set the alarm for seven o'clock and fell sound asleep.

When the alarm went off, my heart dropped. I realized this was it. Strangely, I put my head back down on the pillow, as if to delay what I had waited so long to discover. From across the room, I heard a voice say, "Get up and check the list." I replied, "No way." Then both Lisa and Christa pleaded with me. I gave in and went to the hospitality room.

For a long time I stood and stared at the list. Many times I had worn the USA jersey with dignity and pride. But now, perhaps for one final time, I would do so while representing my country in the Olympic Games.

Unfortunately, the euphoria from having made the team did not cure my injury. The next week, while jogging, I felt a sharp pain in my right shoulder. The next day I went jogging and the pain went from my shoulder down my arm. The third day I went jogging I had to stop and walk because the pain was so bad. That night I couldn't sleep.

I had to sit up at a 90-degree angle in order to even doze off. I couldn't lay flat. I knew right away that I must have a ruptured disc in my back.

I totally lost the strength in my arm and it worried me so much I stopped thinking about the Olympics and started worrying about my career as a doctor. How good would I be without the use of my arm? I prayed a lot in the following weeks.

That's a pretty scary moment as an athlete, when you start thinking about an injury and immediately worry about how it will impact life for you after sports. I wasn't even thinking about softball. It almost seemed like a forgone conclusion that I'd have to give it up. When I lost the strength in my arm, I knew that all the things I took for granted were in jeopardy. I knew it was serious.

I happened to be going to Las Vegas with Lisa the next day and the pain was so bad I had to sit in an awkward position the whole way. Once we got there, I went to see a doctor who kept me there in traction for twelve days.

From there, I went straight to Montana, where my parents were visiting my sister. I needed to be surrounded by my family. I just needed someone to take care of me. Isn't it funny that you always run back to mom and dad when things are tough? It was one of the most painful things ever, and it took me about five days with my parents before I could finally start sleeping through the night.

It was bad, and I didn't want to tell anyone at the hospital about it. I didn't want them to worry about me. I didn't want them to say, ''Oh golly, you have to stop this sport, you know, you're jeopardizing your career.'' I didn't want to tell the Olympic team officials about it either, for fear they'd replace me. Only a few of my teammates knew. I hoped I had plenty of time to get over the pain before I had to play again.

I returned home to Los Angeles for a couple of days, then flew on to Orlando where my parents live. For three months I never jogged. I didn't do anything that could jeopardize my neck. I started working with a physical trainer, who went nuts every time I flew off to do another clinic or to give a speech. She wanted me in the training room, getting better.

I was so weak on the right side I couldn't believe it. As an athlete, you're always testing yourself. After the injury, I was always trying to test myself by holding a bat out straight. I couldn't do it. I ended up straining my bicep tendon trying to do it.

I kept wondering why. I thought it happened so I would be able to understand my patients who come in and have neck problems, and describe how the pain radiates down their arm. Once I learned that, I prayed that it would all go away.

But slowly, after four months with a trainer, my strength all started coming back, though even today I have numbness on the tip of my right thumb, which is a reminder of what I went through.

So all of a sudden I'm feeling stronger. I'm starting to throw the ball the way I did before the injury. That's when I knew I was getting better. When I was hurt, I was throwing the ball as hard as I could and it just didn't seem to go anywhere. But now I was hearing it pop into other people's gloves. It was an incredible feeling, getting my health back. your health is so precious, and when we don't have it, it means so much more when it comes back. We should appreciate it and not take it for granted.

Well, the next thing I knew it was April 15, time to report to Columbus, Georgia, to get ready as a team for the run up to the Olympics in July. There were two of us per apartment there at the training complex, and Lisa was my roommate. Of course I chose the master bedroom. Age before beauty.

I was ready to play. We put on our practice uniforms and, for the first week, went hard at it every day on the practice field. Then they handed us a schedule of exhibition games—sixty of them to be played in towns coast-to-coast between then and the Olympics. I loved interacting with the crowds. I loved signing autographs, taking pictures, and feeling like an ambassador for my sport. But midway through the sixty-game schedule, the players started getting tired of the constant travel, especially the midday two-hour drives to shopping malls for mandated appearances just hours before a game.

But we all knew that we were doing something that no one before us or after us would be able to do. We were bringing the Olympics to the rest of America.

Most games, the competition wasn't that great. The best thing would have been for us to play top college teams, like the women's basketball team did. But the NCAA wouldn't let those teams play us until after June.

The pre-Olympic tour did provide us with some very humorous moments. The first for me came in the second game of the tour in Long Beach, California. ESPN had asked to put a microphone on, so they could tape my chatter throughout the game for a feature story. I remember worrying as I walked to the batter's box for my first at-bat how I would play with the mike on. Then I hit the first pitch thrown to me dead over the center field fence.

Funny, but as I started running around the bases, I really didn't know what to say. I felt I needed to say something monumental, because I was miked. But nothing came to mind. Finally, I just yelled ''Wow!'' That was it. Not too good for television. But it was what came natural. I thought, ''I hope I get wired every game. I can handle this!''

I'm not really much of a home run hitter, so that made the whole moment rather surprising. In fact, I only hit one other home run in the entire pre-Olympic series. That was in Houston, which was a big hit because our team was not hitting the pitcher in that game very well and then all of a sudden I just ripped it. It's my job as the leadoff hitter to set the tone of the game, and most times that wasn't with a home run. When I was named to the Olympic team, we had a meeting with the team leader, Ronnie, who said, ''Dot, you've got to lead us. We're depending on you. With the players that we have chosen, you can see that your international experience is going to be needed in certain areas.'' I took that challenge very seriously every game.

We went 59-1 during that series, losing the second game of a doubleheader in Los Angeles very early on. Michele Granger Paulos had pitched for us against a local team which had some great players on it. They beat us in the bottom of the seventh inning. We were ahead 1-0. They ended up getting two hits and an error, and scored the two runs to win. They were going berserk. I guess I can't blame them. As a team, we decided that was a feeling we never wanted to feel again.

I was bothered by the loss, but not as much as I was bothered by what happened afterward. After most of the games, we stayed around for hours signing autographs. But that night, we stayed thirty minutes, then were swept away. I thought that was bad, because whether you win or lose a game, the message is not victory, the message for these young players is competition at the elite level. And just because you lose a game, that doesn't mean it's an embarrassment or something you feel ashamed about, because in our lives we are all going to lose one time or another. How you handle losing determines whether you're a champion or not, and for me it was an embarrassment that we rushed off after losing. Yes, we were all tired, we needed to get to sleep. But when we won, we were there for three hours. When we lost, we were taken away in thirty minutes. It's not right.

The next day, Coach Raymond said we all looked tired and it was too early in the process for us to be that tired. Some of the players pointed out that our travel schedule had been pretty hectic, but he didn't believe that was the reason. He thought we were spending too much time playing tennis and racquetball after practice in Columbus, so he told us not to do that anymore. It was obvious he meant business.

We played the last game of our tour in Atlanta on July 4 against a Tennessee team that had given us good competition in an earlier game. My only memory of that game is that I wore a knee pad from Rawlings, my personal sponsor, and got yelled at by our association's officials because I wasn't wearing the gear provided by their sponsors. Nothing like that had ever happened to me before, so it really threw me off. I played horribly. I realized that for some folks this wasn't just about the love of the game, and that depressed me.

My brother, Lonnie, who was in the stands, pulled me aside and told me not to let anyone else's feelings stand in the way of what we were there to do. He was right. I can't control where my sport is going or what deals people are making, but I can control my game, between the lines. And there, I'm pretty good.

By the time the last out of that sixtieth game was made, our team had come together. Now it was time, as the announcer would say, to 'Let the games begin!' Our first official act was to participate in the incredible opening ceremonies in Atlanta.

During the opening ceremonies, our team marched with other USA athletes into the stadium and around the track. I felt like we were walking all the way around the world. I just couldn't stop waving at the crowd. My teammates and the other athletes were waving too, and I remember hearing a number of them say, ''God, my arms are sore.'' I couldn't even feel mine. I probably could have kept them up forever.

At one stage, I got so caught up in waving that I forgot to keep walking. The USA team was divided, the women walking first, and the men behind them. Suddenly, as I was looking into the stands and waving to the President— I was waving to the President of the United States!—I looked around and I was surrounded by the men, because

I had fallen so far back in the pack. As I walked around, I looked hard for my mother and brother, who were in the stadium. I found them and let my arms go into overdrives.

Once our lap around the stadium was complete, we were in the infield for the ceremony. It was moving as well. I saw our flag go up and my heart was beating as hard as I thought it could. I felt this strength of brotherhood, and just for a moment it seemed that the whole world was captured in peace and filled with unity. I don't know how to describe it other than to say that I wish every moment of every day could be like this for everyone. The pride, the patriotism, the respect. It was a moment when I was so proud to be human, a part of the human race.

CHAPTER

TEN

Atlanta 1996

One of the toughest things to do in sports is to live up to expectations when you're the favorite. Ask sprinter Michael Johnson. In many ways, our softball team faced the same challenge.

Yet it's the type of pressure that every elite athlete wants. You want to be the best of the best. It's easier to climb to the top than it is to stay there. A lot of people say that the best part of my career is that I have been able to stay at the top for a very long time. For me it wasn't pressure, it was excitement. It was the challenge of challenges and it was at the Olympic games.

Because they couldn't find a site in Atlanta to play the softball championships, our games were played an hour away, in Columbus. To me, that was an advantage. If we had been in the Olympic village in Atlanta, it might have been tough, because we would have been caught up in the awe of the other athletes. We felt it in the opening ceremonies. I think there would have been a lot of distractions in Atlanta. But at our facility, everything was serious;

all the countries had their routines and they were out for gold.

We stayed in the officers' quarters at Fort Benning, and we had a fifteen-minute drive to the fields in Columbus. Because of security concerns, every day we took a different route. The security was awesome. They had guys up on towers watching the whole perimeter. We were in the safest place, and we were treated incredibly well.

When the tournament draw came up, we were to play Puerto Rico in the first game. When we walked out of the dugout, as soon as we were seen, the crowd stood and screamed, and the ovation was unbelievable. It sent chills through your whole body.

Months after I was selected to the team, I had a recurring dream in which I was the leadoff hitter and knocked the first ever Olympic softball pitch out of the park for a home run. I desperately wanted to hit that first homer in Olympic softball history. Not only that, but also in my dream I hit the home run that would win the gold medal for the United States. Talk about a good night's sleep!

When we got into the first game of the Olympics, I was disappointed that we were the home team. Because the visiting team always bats first, the hitters from Puerto Rico got the chance to hit that first pitch I had dreamed about. Well, they got a hit, but not a home run. My dream was still alive.

When I got up in the bottom of the first inning, the first pitch to me was in the dirt. You could see the disappointment on my face, because I didn't even get the chance to swing at it. I was thinking ''This isn't right. Can we start over?'' I was supposed to hit that first pitch for a home run, and it didn't even cross the plate. I got a hit that first time up. But in my fourth at bat, I got the pitch of my dream. I had hit the first home run of the Olympics.

We went on to beat Puerto Rico 10-0, and I realized that while I didn't get a chance to hit the first pitch of the first game out for a home run, my teammate, Michele Granger Paulos, got the chance to throw the first pitch of the Olympics. My home run, it seemed, ignited everything for us—on the field and off. The team continued to strengthen, and excitedly more reporters started showing up to cover our sport.

NBC started showing nightly highlights of our games. We were told before the Olympics that NBC wasn't going to show any of our games. Newspaper and magazine articles were springing up everywhere, some referring to us as the real "Dream Team."

In our second game, against the Netherlands, I hit another home run. This time it came in my second at-bat as we went on to win 9-0. Suddenly, everyone thought I was going to hit a home run every game. Even I was thinking it for a while.

Our third game, against Japan, ended my streak. The win left us as the only undefeated team in the tournament on only the third day. By the time we beat Chinese Taipei in the fourth game, 4-0, we had outscored our first four opponents, 29-1, and had three shutouts. As exciting as our offense was, our defense was better. We appeared to be living up to the expectations of the front-runner.

In our fifth game, against Canada, we won again, 4-2, setting up big games with our two biggest rivals, Australia and China, in the next two days. The toughest part of the

Canada game was that it didn't end until 2:30 A.M. and we had to play Australia the next morning. We got almost no sleep as a team. In fact, when it started raining during the Australia game, our team went back into the locker room, and fell asleep on the floor.

We were tired, but we were also pumped, because we knew Australia was a tough competitor. Lisa was throwing fantastically. I hadn't seen Lisa throw like that since 1991. She wanted it, and it was obvious. We started trying to pick ourselves up, but our bats were a little slow. And when you're facing Australia's Tanya Harding, who is throwing the ball sixty-eight miles an hour, you don't have time to be a little tired. Hitting is so mental, and you can't be anything but sharp against that kind of speed. So we were struggling offensively. But so was Australia.

We were both scoreless going into the fourth inning when Dani Tyler, our third baseman, crushed a shot over the center field wall. I was in the on-deck area near our dugout and the television cameras were right behind me. When I saw Dani's shot, I ducked down low so the cameras could get a good look. It was beautiful. Dani was ecstatic. And as she came home, I watched her step toward home and I remember wondering if she'd clearly stepped on the plate. I was going to say something to her, but I figured no umpire would make that call. The ball went twenty feet over center field fence. I was wrong. I watched Australia protest and the umpire tell our coach, Ralph Raymond, that Dani had missed the plate and was out. I couldn't believe it.

I couldn't believe that Coach didn't go out there and fight. I thought that in a tournament this big, she deserved her moment, she deserved a fight. She deserved someone to be thrown out of the game for that call, even if it was going to be me. When Coach didn't do it, I bolted out of the dugout and headed straight for the umpire. I don't know if it was my role or not, but I took it anyway. I was yelling, "Are you telling me that a girl is going to hit a ball twenty feet over the fence in the Olympic Games and you're going to take it away from her? You're taking her moment away from her? Unbelievable." I never disputed whether she touched it or not. I just wanted to make the point.

Well, the call stood. When I got back to the dugout, Ralph held a quick huddle and started yelling at me. He said, "It's your fault she missed home plate. She should have been concentrating on running the bases, but she was worrying about getting home and celebrating with you. You should stay in the dugout and stop being a coach." I said "Yes, sir" and went to my position. As we were going out, Dani ran by me and told me she understood what was happening, that he had yelled at me because he knew I could take it and he had to yell at someone. She was right.

But Dani got her fight. I gave it to the umpires for her. She knew that we still believed in her. That's what a team is all about. Whether it was right for me to yell at the umpires, I don't know. I've never done it before; my parents were astonished. But I felt it was her moment, she'd earned it. It is sixty feet between each base in softball, 240 feet around the base paths. For 239 feet, she was able to enjoy her moment. I wanted her to have that last foot.

At the end of seven innings the score was still tied, so

we went into extra innings. We scored one run, then they came up. With a runner on second, we had them with two outs and two strikes on the batter, Joanne Brown. Everyone in the bleachers was standing up. They were chanting ''USA, USA.'' We were one strike away from pulling the game out.

But then Joanne Brown put the next pitch dead over the center field fence. My first hope was for Laura Berg to catch it, make some miraculous catch. No chance. The ball was way over the fence. My next thought was for Lisa. I felt bad for her. She had deserved the win. We had let her down.

The stadium was silent with only the few hundred fans for Australia going crazy. When Joanne came home, she jumped up and smashed onto home plate. I felt that was disrespectful and unnecessary, given what had happened to Dani.

So we lost 2-1. However, I really believe it was good for the sport that Australia—which hosts the 2000 Olympics— beat the United States. It sets up a great rivalry, a great game Down Under. Plus, I think it was a good thing for our team. We felt the loss and knew then that it could happen again if we didn't play our best every day. The loss put some doubt in our minds. When you get to a point where you win all the time and you're used to winning, it's a shock when you don't.

But while there were a lot of positives out of that game, I have to be honest. What Ralph said to me that day really hurt for a few days. It stayed with me. I had to make it right. I finally went to him and apologized for yelling at the umpires. He said, ''No, I owe you an apology, I was

wrong. I love you, Tiger." I said "I love you too, Ralph."
It was behind us.

One of the things I was proudest of was that after the
game, no one blamed Dani for the loss. We were all professional enough to know that in sports, anything can happen.
Yes, Dani should have hit the center of home plate, but
she didn't. Each of us at one point in our life has made a
mistake. Besides, teams win or lose *together.*

We beat China the next day and moved into the medal
round. That win was important, because had we lost, we
would have been third or fourth in the medal round, which
would have added an extra game to our path to the gold
medal. With all that on the line, we were losing 1-0 after
China hit a home run off Michelle Smith. I was thinking,
"No, not again," because Australia hit a home run to beat
us and you just don't see too many home runs hit off our
pitchers. Well, Sheila Cornell came to the rescue, hitting
a home run off a change-up with a runner on, to win 2-1.
It was a great hit, a key play for Sheila and for the team.

By winning against China, we were the first seed in the
medal tournament despite the loss to Australia. China was
the second seed. Australia was third. Japan was fourth.
The way it worked, 1 plays 2 and 3 plays 4. The loser of
the 3-4 game is out. The winner plays the loser of the 1-
2 game.

Well, we beat China for the second time in as many
days, sending us directly to the gold medal game. I was
frustrated in that game, because China's pitchers seemed
to have my number, striking me out for the second time
on breaking balls. This time I struck out with the bases
loaded. It got to the point that I went to my parents for a

little advice. Mom knew that I rarely struck out, so she tried to encourage me by telling me there had to be a reason for what was happening. She's such an optimist. I said, ''Yeah, it's happening because they're going to throw me a change-up in the gold medal game and I'm gonna put it over the fence.'' No kidding, I said that. And that's what ended up happening.

Our win over China sent them into the loser's bracket game against Australia. The winner of China-Australia was going to be our opponent for the gold medal. Everyone kept asking us who we wanted to play for the gold medal: Australia, who had beaten us in the controversial game, or China, considered by most people the second-best team in the world, behind us. Beating China three times—beating anyone three times—is tough to do, and would solidify our place as the dominant team.

Me, I didn't care whom we played. In my mind, the gold medal was our destiny, and no one was going to get in our way.

CHAPTER

ELEVEN

After the Gold

While standing on the gold medal podium, I remember thinking, "It doesn't get any better than this." Well, I was wrong. I have been consistently surprised at how many times I've said that since.

After the award presentations, I was told Bob Costas wanted to do a live interview with the team. I was the one chosen to round-up everyone. The catch was I only had five minutes to gather my teammates. Not an easy task, given that they were enjoying the moment with family and friends. Once we were on the air, it was a tremendous opportunity to share the emotions we were feeling with the rest of America.

I was astonished at the number of cameras and media people milling about the field. Reporters were everywhere, and I couldn't help but feel that the world had fallen in love with the sport we'd loved all our lives. There was the sense of excitement, achievement, and pride.

After the interviews, I was told there was a little girl back in the stadium who had been waiting this whole time for my autograph. I ran back onto the field. I looked everywhere but no one was around. The roar of the crowd was now silent and all that remained was the memories.

As I turned to walk back to the locker room, I heard a loud yell from the outfield, "Olympic Gold Baby!" Quickly, I looked up into the right field bleachers and there were four girls. They couldn't have been more than fourteen years old. When our eyes met, they cried out again even louder, "OLYMPIC GOLD BABY!" These were the words I had so often used in the softball clinics I had been doing throughout the country. It was a phrase used to let the athlete know she was doing things correctly.

Immediately, I raised the gold medal to them saying, "OLYMPIC GOLD BABY! NOW, GO GET YOURS!!!"

There was a celebration party for family and friends being held at the Whisperwood Apartments. All of our families and friends were there. It was a very special time filled with emotion. I will never forget the looks on everyone's faces when they got to hold and wear the gold medal. I found myself saying (once again), "It doesn't get any better than this." When I saw the gold medal on Mom and Dad, I knew that was where it belonged.

My closest friends were also at the party: Kaelyn, Michael, Jeff, Tom and his wife Heather. I was so glad they all lived it with me. They have always been there for me throughout the years. And tonight was no exception. They will never know how proud I am of them and how much it meant to have them with me at the Olympics.

I reflected on all who may not have been on the field with us, but were there in our thoughts. I thought about

Allyson Rioux. How much she would have loved to have been a part of this.

When the party had concluded at around 2:30 A.M., some of my teammates and I flew to Atlanta to do a live interview on *The Today Show*. At one point, each of us was asked what our plans were now that the games were over. Some mentioned how much they were looking forward to attending closing ceremonies, celebrating, or taking a vacation.

Then it was my turn, ''I'm going to Walt Disney World—NOT! I'm going back to L.A. to work.'' The Olympics were now over for me.

I had one quick stop to make before going to the airport. Reebok, Inc. wanted me to come by their facility. When I arrived they showered me with apparel and took me on a short tour. Reebok, Inc. had previously signed Lisa Fernandez. It had to have been a proud moment for them. They were a company who'd believed in our sport and in the athletes who participated in it. During the tour, I noticed there were posters on the walls of their top endorsed athletes. I couldn't help but notice our sport was missing. Hopefully, with time that too will change.

It was time to head to the airport. It would be a flight that would bring me back to a world I never imagined or even dared to dream about.

On the way to the airport, we stopped at the NBC headquarters where Jon Frankel, one of their reporters, was waiting with a plane ticket. He informed me that he was going to accompany me to the airport. He explained that he had done a number of interviews with the softball players and had fallen in love with our team. There was another car following us with all the cameras, and I thought he just wanted to get a picture of us going to the airport. When I got out of the car, people rushed over and swarmed around the car, wanting my autograph. They were taking pictures and yelling for me to pose. Then we walked inside, rushing to make the flight. I couldn't find my ticket anywhere. My spirit sank when I saw that there were at least a hundred people in the ticket line. Suddenly, everyone in line turned around and started clapping. They were yelling and whistling for me. I was overwhelmed. One of the American Airline supervisors grabbed me and escorted me to the metal detector. I stepped through and all the alarms went off. I reached in and pulled out the gold medal, and everyone started clapping and cheering and whistling all over again. *The Today Show* crew was taping the whole thing, and I was just blown away. I had never been recognized before by people I had never seen or met.

I signed pictures and autographed cards and shook hands until they called our flight, then we were escorted to the first-class section. I knew there had to be a mistake because I had never before flown in first class. I couldn't believe it. The flight attendant came over and told me that there were dozens of people in the coach section that wanted autographs, so I stood in between the first-class and coach sections, taking pictures, signing autographs, and putting the gold medal on people's necks all the way to Dallas!

When we landed in Dallas two and a half hours later, I was swept onto one of those carts that carry people who have difficulty walking. I've always secretly wanted to take a ride on one of those. The driver said, "Hang on,

Dot!'' and off we sped, going superfast down through the terminal. I noticed people stopping to stare, and heard them say, ''Oh my gosh, that is the Doctor. That's Doctor Dot!''

I could not believe that people all the way in Dallas knew who I was. We boarded the plane to L.A. and it started all over again. I was exhausted with all the exhilaration of the day, and I fell asleep in my seat. The last thing I remember hearing before I drifted off was the overhead speakers crackling, ''Dr. Dot is so tired, but she promises to sign all of your autographs in L.A.''

I had been living in Columbus for four months in preparation for the Olympics, and had given up my apartment, so I had no place to live when I returned to L.A. Kaelyn and Michael had an extra bedroom, so I went to their house. That night, Jon and I did *The Today Show* interview from their house. We finished late and I knew I had to get some sleep. I had a five o'clock morning radio interview to do, then I had to go to work.

I reported to the orthopedic floor and was met by one of the organizing executives at the hospital, Tom Welch. Tom was chosen to brief me on everything that was planned on the teams for the day, and explained that I had been moved from sports medicine and assigned to trauma. One of my colleagues had dropped out of the program and they were short. It suddenly hit me that the greatest lesson I had learned in sports was also important in medicine and in life: teamwork. I had to jump in and do what the team needed me to do, although I wasn't expecting it. However, before I started my shift, Tom said that I needed to attend the press conference. He escorted me down to administration, and to my surprise, everyone was there. The chief of surgery, the residents, the doctors, the nurses. People were gathering in the hallways. The emotion was incredible! The hugs, the smiles, the tears, as I walked to the podium and faced the cameras. A USC marching band was playing the Olympic theme song, and some 800 people were cheering and pointing. I turned away from the cameras and looked behind me to see a huge banner that read, "CONGRATULATIONS DR. DOT RICHARDSON. WELCOME BACK!

I was speechless. I knew I was supposed to say something, but I was overcome with emotion. They gave me a plaque, and I experienced an unbelievable closeness with these people. It was more than just sharing the Olympic dream, these were the people I lived and worked with. In the health field, the demands are so stringent and you love as much as you can, but there are so many moments of trying and testing.

We had all been in it together, a team, and they were with me a 100 percent. I could feel them with me during the competitions and now we were actually getting to share it together. I passed the medal around to everyone that was there, and just hugged people. I cried. I lived the moment to the fullest.

It was a funny sight when we went back into the hospital and noticed that the benches, normally filled with hundreds of patients, were inhabited by NBC, ESPN, CNN, and CBS. I did interviews with all of them, and they actually talked to some patients who agreed to be on TV. I spent the whole day with the media and was worn out by the end. After it was finally over, I was notified that the department had decided to give me another week off to go meet the President at the White House, be a guest on the David

Letterman show, and participate in the Walt Disney World parade.

Instead of leaving right away, I decided I wanted to go to the Children's Hospital. I wanted to make sure that every one of those kids had that gold medal around their necks. We were followed by people in the hospital who took Polaroids of every kid wearing the gold medal. We were in the wellness ward, with kids who were getting better. I gave a little talk to them, shared some of my dreams, and talked about the Olympics while we hung the medal around their necks. Then we went to the bedsides of patients who could not come to the wellness ward, then finally to the bottom floor: the intensive care units. These were the really sick patients. I saw this little boy whose temperature was around 103 and who was not doing very well. I hung the medal around his neck and he rewarded me with a smile.

The last patient I saw was a beautiful little girl about ten years old. She had just had brain surgery four days earlier. She was bald on one side of her head from the surgery, and had strands of black hair on the other. I introduced myself to her mother and her sister, then I gently hung the gold medal around her neck. I leaned in very close to her, so that our heads touched. Someone snapped the Polaroid, and I stepped back to show it to her. "You look good in gold," I told her. She startled me by responding, "Is it really gold?" Her mother and sister started crying hysterically as I left the room, as did the nurses. I grabbed the nurse closest to me and asked what was wrong? "You don't understand," she sobbed. "This little girl has not spoken a word since her surgery."

Could anything be more priceless than that Olympic gold medal then? More important than the Olympic medal itself was the opportunity to share it and make a difference in the lives of others. It was never more evident than in that trip to the hospital. Those kids were inspired, they were motivated, they lived a small part of it with me, but most of all, they realized they could live their dreams. It was a reality check for me.

I finally got to go home to Florida. Walt Disney World had asked me to be in their parade and had invited me to stay at the Yacht Club. I gratefully declined the Yacht Club because I wanted to stay with my mom and dad. I had left so abruptly to drive to Columbus, and I had not gotten to say good-bye, much less had time to visit with them. When we arrived at Disney World for the parade event, the valet parking guys recognized me. What a thrill in my home state! They escorted me inside and gave me the key to the Captain's Galley. The entrance had a chandelier and there were full-length mirrors all around. The table sat fourteen people, and the den had a huge TV. The living room had sliding glass doors that opened into my very own garden with a pool. The bedroom was fit for a queen, with a huge bed and walk-in closets bigger than my whole bedroom at home! The bathroom had gigantic showers and there was a phone next to the toilet. I had a kitchen with a refrigerator and everything. It was the most glamorous place I ever stayed. Of course, I ran back into the main bedroom and jumped on the bed. I immediately called Mom and Dad and said, ''You have got to get over here!'' The word spread to my sisters and my brothers and their families. I already had my brother Lonnie and his family there, and Michael and Kaelyn. Walt Disney World ended up giving us five extra rooms to accommodate everyone.

My favorite place in the world other than my parents' house is Walt Disney World. I grew up there. It offers you a chance to be young again, to be where everything in life is good. It makes you feel so alive.

The David Letterman show was a blast. We went out in the street and he pitched to me. I hit the balls everywhere on the streets of New York. One hit a car, another rolled over some trash cans.

Then I went to the White House and got to meet the President. That was the most incredible feeling. There were all of the USA delegates for the Olympics in the White House backyard. The Rose Garden. I could see the Washington Monument and the Lincoln Memorial, and I was so proud to have represented the United States and given it all we could. I thought to myself, "It doesn't get any better than this." It was just breathtaking. There were interviews going on all around me, and they announced the arrival of the President. There were thousands of cameras and we lined up in rows. I was in the fourth or fifth row in the middle. The President walked in with his daughter, Chelsea, followed by Hillary. I was filled with pride as I listened to the President speak, knowing that I was in the heart of our country.

Afterward, one of the volleyball players, Linda Robinson, said to me, "How does it feel to be the sweetheart of the Olympics?" I looked at her, stunned, and said you are kidding. She just laughed and replied, "You're the sweetheart, haven't you noticed?" I really couldn't say anything.

Then Hillary spoke, and when she was done, all three of them, the President, Hillary, and Chelsea walked over to us. The President came directly to me and said, "I've been looking forward to meeting you." I turned around and looked behind me to see who he was talking to. He was talking to me! Then Hillary said, "I've got to give you a copy of the column I wrote this morning. I talked about you in it." I was speechless.

We stood there for pictures, and I put my right hand on his left shoulder, and my left hand on her right shoulder. I was right there in the middle. I continued to thank him, and we talked. I really felt like I was imagining the whole thing. I felt like I was Forrest Gump, like someone had just lifted me into the present.

I had to run to the bathroom before we left, so I got directions and slipped off. I found myself in the White House bathroom. I had to be able to say I was really in the White House bathroom, so I took a paper towel with the official presidential seal on it.

I was feeling larger than life as we were waiting to be individually introduced to the President. It seemed like forever before the marine guarding him called out, "Dr. Dot Richardson." I walked over to the President. I signaled for him to bend down, and I put my medal around his neck. I shook his hand and I thanked him again on behalf of L.A. county and also on behalf of the United States Olympic Team. While we were still shaking hands, we turned for a picture. As we turned back, I noticed that his eyes were teary. He took the medal off and gave it back to me. I said hello to Chelsea and then to Hillary Clinton. I put the medal over her neck as well, and we shook hands. She whispered to me that if I ever needed anything, just to call. I thanked her for all of her support, then added that if she ever needed me she knew how to find me too. Our picture was taken and she gave me a huge hug.

I walked into the next room, where there was a huge portrait of Abraham Lincoln. I broke down and bawled my eyes out. It was the such an overwhelming, patriotic, meaningful moment. It's what it all was about. Mary Ellen Clark, the Olympic diver, came into the room and she broke down, too.

The emotion was compounded by the thought that for the first time in international competition, there were presidents, first ladies, and athletes wanting pictures with softball players. It had always been us just reaching to get pictures with basketball or volleyball players in the Olympics, or in the Pan-American or World competitions. But now, for the very first time, it was us that everyone wanted pictures with.

I was the last to leave the White House. Even the guards wanted pictures. When I finally walked out, I had to rush to get into the bus. As we drove away and I looked back at the White House, I felt that we had represented our country well, we had given it our all, and was ultimately proud that it resulted in bringing the first gold medal in softball home to the White House.

I think that what has happened most since the Olympics, from patients recognizing me to being able to share the Olympic gold in clinics, speaking engagements, schools, and business groups, the greatest accomplishment of all has been that people have told me they lived my dream *with* me during the games. In the interview with Bob Costas after the gold game, he said that every time I was on TV, people could always see the true love of the sport in me. That told me I had accomplished every goal I had coming into Atlanta: To compete in the Olympics, to be there representing my country and the athletes before me, and to allow everyone to get caught up in the moment.

To this day, people tell me they felt the excitement of the Olympics just by watching us play. People have said they could sense what it was like to achieve one's highest goal by watching how we celebrated. If that's true—if people were able to live the dream with us—then we were true Olympians.

CHAPTER

TWELVE

Role Models

My parents have always provided a firm foundation for me. They are a large part of why I am where I am today. Growing up, they never treated any one of their children differently than another, yet we all knew we were loved unconditionally. I always knew that my parents would support me in anything I decided to do, and they left me free to make my own choices. Mom and Dad have always been there for me—I know they always will.

My dad would frequently take the time off of work to come and watch me play. My mom was always there even when my dad couldn't get off work, but usually both would be at the game. Even my grandparents would come to my games. Everyone in the stands would know my parents and grandparents. They knew my parents were the ones who drove their mobile home to all the big tournaments and national championships.

I have always called my mom and dad every Sunday, but now that I have a car phone I can call them on the way to work in the mornings too.

My entire family has been so supportive. I have two older sisters, an older brother, and a younger brother. What a blessing it is to have such a strong family that loves to spend time together. We all have Christmas and Thanksgiving together every year. I have missed some of the family reunions because I have been in school so much. When I do get home, it is a special time. We all get together and go out to eat, then congregate at either Mom's, Laurie's, Kenny's, or Lonnie's house.

I have ten nieces and nephews, whom I have gotten to spend a lot of quality time with. I've been fortunate in that I have been able to share my life with them. I try to teach them everything I can. Though I am away so often, I share all my travels with them. They learn geography by following my schedule of interviews and games.

One of my sisters has been divorced and was a single mom for five years before remarrying. I have learned that being a single parent doesn't mean you cannot have a happy, well-adjusted family. As a matter of fact, it is often better for a child to have one parent who loves them and gives herself to them, than to have two parents who don't. Those kids have grown up to be independent and competent, and they have strong leadership qualities. They do not feel like they have missed out on anything because they have had more love than they could ever want. It is not how much time you spend with the children; children need quality time and guidance. That was a huge lesson for me.

Another woman I admire tremendously is my coach, Marge Ricker. Marge taught me so much. At first I had trouble calling her by her first name. She was a lot older and it seemed more appropriate to call her Ms. Ricker or Coach Ricker. She insisted on everyone calling her Marge. She taught me a lot about really expressing who you are through sports. For example she never tried to tone me down. She never stopped me from jumping to get into the batter's box, or from firing the ball around when I got excited about making an out. I would really throw it around with emotion and she never hindered that. She never said you shouldn't be loud or you shouldn't cheer. She always let me just go and do it, and that taught me that it is O.K. to be who I am, and it is important not to try to fit in the mold of someone else. She is very disciplined. She lets you know exactly when practice is starting and exactly when you need to be there. She has a strict schedule.

She taught me that in order to accomplish things, you need to be able to manage the responsibilities. You must first organize responsibilities, and then perform as well. She also taught me that once you step on the field nothing else exists except what you are doing in between the lines, something that is hard to develop because it requires experience. Experience to help you ignore life's distractions, like a fight with your boyfriend, an upcoming exam, or a quarrel with your parents. She also knew how to handle pressure. I learned how to respect a coach from her. I never questioned a coach's call or any of their decisions. They ran the show and I was the player who was there to perform.

With Marge, you always knew she believed in you. You can imagine how important that was to a twelve-year-old bat girl who had been allowed to play on an adult team. In 1981, we were at the Warren Team Invitational in

Houston, Texas. The same field would host the National Championship a month later. It was about 115 degrees on the field and we were playing a tournament. We were going into the second game of the day, and suddenly every muscle in my body started twitching. I lay down in the dugout, but I was sweating profusely and felt terribly fatigued. I tried to walk up the stairs to run onto the field and my legs gave out on me. I sat down on the steps for a few seconds, then I got up and tried again. Marge had always taught us to hustle, so I would normally run out to shortstop position at top speed. Now my legs were giving out, so I started walking. The first play was a ground ball hit to me. I fielded the ball and threw toward first, then my body collapsed to the ground. I looked up to see if the throw got there and it did, the girl was out, but everyone in the stands was silent. They had seen me fall on the ground and they did not know what had happened. I did not know what had happened either.

Marge ran out of the dugout over to me, and asked if I was O.K. I picked myself up and told her that I did not know what was going on. She knew it was from the heat. My body couldn't give anymore.

She told me that if she had someone else to put in the game for me she would, but there was nobody left on the bench.

I told her not to worry, because we were going to score and win the game our next time up to bat. During the next inning we had three runners on with two outs, and guess who is up at bat? I stepped into the box and my body was shaking. The first pitch was a perfect strike but I had a twinge in my arm and my body would not move. I stepped out of the box. Marge called me over to the third base coaches box. Although we only had thirty seconds together, it was one of the most emotional moments of my life. She told me that of all the players she had ever coached, I was the one she would choose to be up at bat right now. What a feeling to have someone you admire express that much faith in you! I stepped back into the batter's box and ripped the next pitch right up the middle. I knew if I had to crawl I would do so to get to first base. I was running as hard as I could, but my muscles just would not respond. I made it to first base before totally collapsing. The runners scored and we won.

It has always reminded me of the power of faith, and the power of having someone believe in you.

After the game, they loaded me up with water and put me in an ice bath. I think it was heat exhaustion. We had another game that night and I played again. And just as Marge believed, we won the championship.

Another role model who helped shape me not just as an athlete but as a person is Ralph Raymond, my coach with the Brakettes, who also coached me in a number of international competitions—including the Olympics.

Ralph is one of the best motivators I've ever been around. He's a strong Christian, a strong family man and he's one of the strongest coaches I've ever had. I say that because he believes in his players so much that they automatically believe in themselves. He expects only your best and he knows that's what he's going to get. No more, no less.

He is the winningest coach in the history of modern sports. I didn't know that until I read it in a magazine.

He's won more games, by percentage, than any other coach in any other sport. John Wooden, Lombardi, anyone.

Basically, his success stems from his ability to attract quality players. He reaches for those who strive to perform at their highest level, and then they deliver for him. He has had fantastic talent play for him, and he knew how to keep people with talent happy. That's not easy all the time. He did it by challenging us without writing goals on a chalkboard. He surrounded himself with people who shared his inner drive.

More importantly, with Ralph, you knew you were part of a family. He taught me how to lead without being a dictator. He did it through presence. You respected him so much that you wanted to please him. That's why he has won eighteen national championships and every international competition he's coached in.

Ralph was in the minor leagues in baseball. He never made it to the big leagues, but that didn't stop him from telling us stories. We all listened intently, even though we had never heard of any of the guys he was talking about. He would bring up examples of all these guys that we never even heard about.

Maybe because he's a man coaching a woman's team, he never treated us the way a lot of coaches do. He never got involved in our personal lives unless we went to him with a problem. He kept it strictly business, which meant we all knew there were no excuses with Ralph. He didn't play someone because he didn't want them to be upset. He gave everyone a shot during the season, then in big games and national championships he went with the players he felt were the best.

Ralph taught me that there might be teammates, whom you didn't get along with or whom you didn't really care about off the field, but when you step on the field you respect each other. He never had low expectations because we were women. Sometimes that happens with coaches who are afraid to set high goals for their players because they think, "Oh they're girls, I have to handle them with kid gloves." Not Ralph. And that was his best quality. He respected our talents as athletes.

Ralph has often told me not to stay in the sport too long. He didn't want it to cost me my career. He preferred that I focus on medicine, a career choice he was proud of me for making. I loved that about him. He could have been selfish as a coach and said differently, but he always pushed us to do our best in every field of life.

He told me there was no way to make money in softball, so I should move on. Yet once it was announced that we were going to be in the Olympics, he personally called, and encouraged me to go for it. He said that he was considering giving the game up until the announcement was made. He had always dreamed of winning the Olympics, too. This was also a big opportunity for him.

As I have looked to others for inspiration and guidance, I feel privileged and proud that others might see me in a similar light. I don't categorize myself as a role model, because I believe only other people can give you that label. Only others can decide if your accomplisments are worth aspiring to.

I am reminded of the athlete that I admired as a young

girl—Chris Evert. When I saw her on television, she was everything I thought was perfect: athletic, talented, pretty, intelligent.

Even though she was not at the pinnacle of women's sports, her success and notoriety were not confined to the tennis courts. While her prowess with a racquet made her a legend, it never escaped my notice that Chris also used her fame to help make a difference in the lives of others. She taught me that our gender didn't have to be a barrier to success; anything we wanted from life, we could have it through determination and perseverance.

I was so impressed with Chris Evert that I went out and bought a "Chris Evert Racquet" and even tried out for the high school tennis team. I was in tenth grade and had never played tennis before, but that wasn't going to stop me. I knew I would be lucky just to make the team, and surprisingly, was chosen as our team's number one singles and number one doubles player. I never really got far with tennis, but I always followed Chris' career.

Unlike most people, I actually had the opportunity to meet my role model. I met Chris in 1995 when we were both honored at a banquet. I did not tell her just how much she had inspired me, but I certainly hope she knows how many lives she's touched.

What Chris Evert was to me, I would like to be for girls and boys today. I would love to be able to inspire others to achieve their dreams because I know since my childhood that once inspired you are never the same. You feel you can accomplish anything. It all becomes real and obtainable.

Certainly, I'm of the opinion that the lessons learned from athletics are ones that help us prepare for the challenges of life. Through the competitive atmosphere that sports creates, you can find out more about yourself and the world around you. How do you handle failure? After an error on the field or in life, are you determined to learn from it and work hard to avoid repeating it, or do you want to hide and drown in the negatives? Are you afraid of failure, or are you afraid of success? All of us go through the good and bad times that make up our lives. It is in sport where you learn how to face them.

As often as possible, I suggest that people train themselves to think positively. In every sport, whenever an athlete achieves victory, someone else is experiencing defeat. We cannot always be on the winning team. I've found that there is usually more to be learned from our setbacks than from our successes. When we truly learn from our failures, then that itself is a victory and should be viewed as such.

It's difficult to explain the mental aspect of the game and the determination it requires; it demands that we learn to bounce back from defeat. When I was fifteen years old and playing in a game for the Orlando Rebels, the bases were loaded at the bottom of the seventh inning. I made one error that cost us the entire game.

Afterwards, I was bawling in the backseat of the car while Mom and Dad drove me home. Quietly, Dad pulled to the side of the road and stopped the car. Turning around to face me, he asked, "Why are you crying?" I sobbed, "Dad, you were there, you saw the whole thing. I lost the game. I should have fielded the ball and thrown the runner out, but I didn't and I lost the game for us."

Dad's response was a simple one. "When you are on

the field, you either do it or you don't. Tonight you just didn't do it. That's all there is to it.''

I still remember that simple bit of wisdom that he gave me, and I call on it often. It opened my eyes and I realized that he was exactly right. In all aspects of life, you may only have one chance, one opportunity to make the play or to make a difference. You either do it or you don't. If you don't do it, then learn from it and prepare yourself for the next time.

Though impossible, I would relish the opportunity to help every single athlete out there. That's why I take the time to do softball clinics, speaking appearances, and instructional video tapes. I enjoy sharing the fundamentals of the sport along with the secrets of my success.

I find an inner satisfaction from sharing with others. If I could give to another and make a difference in just one person's life, then my life would have been worth living. That is the type of person I would want to be; helping others enjoy the things I have been so blessed to enjoy.

When I looked in the crowd at the Olympics, I saw my niece Alison Parker leaning over the rail. She is fifteen and plays softball in Orlando. Ever since she was nine she has had an unbelievable desire to play and a love of the sport. In fact, she is in my first instructional video tape. When she leaned over to hug me, I saw such pride and inspiration on her face. I could see it in everyone. I thought, ''This day is for you and so many like you.''

When asked what the most memorable part of the Olympics was, I think every reporter expected to hear, ''Being on the podium and receiving the gold medal.'' But truly, the most memorable moment was when I saw the looks on people's faces in the crowd. At that moment, they knew that they, too, could capture their "golds" in life.

I was excited for all those young athletes. I want them to go all the way and I want to experience it with them. You know, those people who dare to achieve are usually those people who are motivated from within. True motivation is found inside yourself; neither I or anyone else can teach it. It takes hard work and dedication, and a love for what you are doing to reach those goals you set for yourself.

I like to ask young athletes why they play the sport. For the girls in softball, it obviously isn't for money. Some say to get an athletic scholarship. I hope the primary reason is because they love it! So many of the college athletes today are not as driven as student/athletes used to be.

I wonder if that is a result of our pushing them while they are young to get athletic scholarships. That becomes their goal and motivation. Tragically, the love of the sport is often lost along the way. The sport becomes a burden. Today, too many athletes seem focused on peripheral aspects: their own personal performance, their chances for a scholarship, future financial rewards.

A fact often overlooked is that the athletes who earn the scholarships and win championships are the ones who love the sport. The thrill for them lies not in the endorsement possibilities, but in the thrill of simply lacing up their cleats. I love watching those who, despite the immense salaries, have not lost their fire or love of the game.

Michael Jordan and Wayne Gretzky are marquee players who exude this quality. Perhaps the best ever in their respective sports, I can guarantee you that big money contracts were never the motivation behind their successes.

When I watch them play, it's clear that they love the game like they did as children.

Many kids today don't realize that when I played at UCLA, we never got free Reebok cleats. The big news while I was there was we got our first ever free uniforms. It seems as though too many young athletes only see the glamourous side of sports: head coaches flying in and catering to athletes, taking them out to dinner and treating them like royalty.

I am happy for anyone who can make a living playing a sport; I wish I'd had the opportunity to do that. That's where male athletes at the highest level have always had an advantage. So, like most female athletes, I found a career that gave me a similar feeling as athletics. In medicine, everyday is like winning the gold medal. For me, there is no greater reward than to give of yourself to others, to help heal them in their time of need.

It's difficult to compare working in a hospital as an underpaid resident to being a professional athlete earning millions. But it is society that has chosen the professional athlete as someone whose contribution is worthy of a higher salary. It is this message that is regularly missed by many athletes. They're not aware of their influence upon society, and that they could use their impact to give something back to those that idolize them. I firmly believe that with our good fortunes as athletes, there come responsibilities.

Jackie Joyner-Kersee is a woman who understands this. She has set a marvelous example for her contribution and dedication to improving the neighborhood she grew up in. People like her should be admired for their selflessness; in my mind, Jackie is an exemplary role model.

What every athlete, politician, movie or television star must realize is that whether we want to be or not, we are role models. So rather than deny it, we should step up and recognize that there may be one person out there who thinks you are worth their attention. That in itself is something special.

Many parents don't realize that everyday their child looks to them and sees them in this light. You make an impact in the development of your child. You pass on to them your beliefs and your ideals. You make the choice of how you would like to influence another. Hopefully, all of us realize we are role models. There are just some who are more famous than others.

And while I believe most athletes enjoy the challenge of being a role model, it is unfortunate that the headlines are dominated by the players who spit on umpires, make obscene gestures to the crowd or kick television cameramen. The positive actions of people like Jackie are overshadowed by the negative ones of a few. This is where the media can make a difference if they choose to.

Recently, there was a high school player who punched a referee in the face. How can we tell him that his behavior is wrong when the media continues to focus upon professionals who have done worse?

America's big corporations have a chance to make a difference by whom they seek as endorsers. Often, endorsements are given to athletes who enjoy reputations as being less than sportsmanlike. I find this disappointing because the corporations are rewarding, and therefore advocating, that sort of behavior. Corporations respond to this problem with the answer, "It sells!" Certainly, society has confirmed the marketability of such attitudes, but I wonder if companies consider what they're encouraging young children to imitate.

After the Olympics, I was approached with the concept of doing a movie about my life pursuing a gold medal. But after the writer spent some time with me, there was a question about whether they could actually get the movie to the screen because there was not enough "conflict" in my life. No alcohol problems, no drug abuse, no addiction, no child abuse, no prostitution. Since I didn't have to overcome those things, my story wasn't controversial or interesting enough to get attention. They also maintained that there is little market for movies that feature successful women.

I would not be terribly upset if the project fell through. I understand that controversial movies have built-in publicity value. However, I find it difficult to believe that society has deteriorated to the point where only a few of us find pleasure in watching others succeed, regardless of the central character's gender.

I have an unshakeable belief in the goodness of people, and that we all have a responsibility to help one another. My mother and father, Marge Ricker, Ralph Raymond, Jackie Joyner-Kersee—these are all people who share this philosophy. Along with so many others, they inspired, taught, and pushed me to become the person I am; in short, they are my role models. And if I can emulate them and perhaps help others in a similar fashion, then I believe I have partially fulfilled my responsibility not only as a successful athlete, but also as a human being.

CHAPTER

THIRTEEN

The Business of Sport

There is no denying the fact that the sales of athletic merchandise is a huge business, not only in this country but around the globe. Companies endlessly battle each other to create new products, and then spend billions of dollars hiring well-known sports personalities to convince the public that their cleats, or gloves, or bats are simply the best.

It has certainly been a struggle to get female athletics recognized. And among women's sports, I can assure you that softball is not one of the higher profile ones. Up until recently, Lisa Fernandez and I were the only softball players to retain the services of an agent. Previously, there just wasn't a need.

I have included this chapter to help all those who may find themselves in the position Lisa and I were in just a few years ago, when we were both approached with the first real endorsement possibilities for softball. I hope all can learn from Lisa's wisdom and from my naiveté.

It all started with bats. A few years ago, I became very

frustrated with my inability to find a bat I really liked. All that I tried were either too heavy or too long.

Before a doubleheader one evening, a fan called me over to the fence. He had with him this beautiful blue bat. He asked me to try it out in the games. At this point, I was willing to try anything! That night I went seven for eight. The ball seemed to bounce right off the bat. I liked it. I went to give the bat back after the game, but this gentleman wouldn't take it. He said to keep it and use it for the rest of the season. I thanked him and thought it was a great idea.

Little did I know, but this man had videotaped my performance and brought it back to the manufacturer. They must have liked what they saw because the next weekend the same guy came up to me and invited me for a visit to the manufacturer's plant. I graciously accepted the invitation. That Monday, I met the president of the company. I really didn't know what to expect but everyone was great and I deeply felt I could trust them.

So at the end of my visit, I signed my first contract. It was the first bat contract of a female softball player that I am aware of. The agreement included the first signature bat to be signed by a woman.

My rommate, Lisa Fernandez, had just come off of her senior year at UCLA and was working on a contract with Louisville Slugger. She was introduced to a lawyer who was representing her in the negotiations for a bat and glove contract. It was taking a long time for the negotiations, but things looked promising. This was huge news, not just for women softball players but for all women athletes. I was excited for her and the opportunities this would mean for others. I was also excited about my new found opportunities and the doors it might open.

When I got back to our apartment later that day, I told Lisa that I had signed a contract. She thought that I shouldn't have done so without legal representation. She was right, of course, but in the meantime I was still enthused about how history was being made between the two of us and our sport. We were breaking new ground.

Lisa and Louisville Slugger had come to an agreement. After this, she was directed to a sports agent, Tom McCarthy, of Progressive Sports Management, Inc., who was based out of Temecula, California. I could see the exciting opportunities that were developing for her through his efforts. Together they broke new ground again by signing for apparel with Reebok International, Ltd.

At one of my appearances at a sporting goods show in Chicago, I was introduced to one of the top businessmen at Rawlings® Sporting Goods. I was excited by the prospect of being a part of such a well-respected company. I have always used and loved my Rawlings glove, and I very much hoped that we could come to some sort of endorsement agreement. We had a great conversation and the result was that they were very interested in me.

When I returned from the trip, I thought I should get myself an agent to help if any negotiations developed. Especially since I was working at the hospital, I didn't have a lot of time. I definitely would need someone to represent me.

I'll never forget the day I called Tom McCarthy. I was

in a rush at the hospital and had only a few minutes to spare. I called him on one of the pay phones across from the cafeteria. I didn't know what to expect, but when Tom answered the phone, there was something in his voice that put me at ease. I introduced myself to him. I explained that I was Lisa's roommate and thought he was doing a great job with her and our sport. I also informed him of the Rawlings® situation and inquired if he would represent me. After talking for a while, Tom said he would love to work with Rawlings® on my behalf.

While it would be a long time before we came to an agreement with Rawlings®, the event was important because it marked the beginning of my relationship with Tom. I realized he and I saw a lot of issues in the same light. He had vision, integrity, and a commitment to make a difference. He represented two softball players when no one else would even consider it. Money couldn't have been his motivation, because outside of tennis, golf, and professional volleyball, the market for female athletes was slim indeed.

It is only recently that corporations have learned that softball is a sport long over-looked in terms of its marketing potential. Louisville Slugger was the first major company to put out a full campaign in the promotion of women's softball. When they signed their marquee player, Lisa Fernandez, and came out with her signature bat, they rediscovered that half of the world population is female, and we sure love to spend money. This was seen in the popularity of the Fernandez bat. The biggest message from the sales of the product was that girls did care about what name was on their sporting equipment. It was evident that girls wanted female role models that they could recognize and look up to.

Tom continued his interest in representing me. It was now only a week before the final tryout for the USA Olympic softball team. I had discussed with Tom about how unhappy I had been with my first bat contract. Nobody could find my bat. In fact, I had to sell it to people out of the trunk of my car.

Tom knew my frustrations. He suggested I write a proposal indicating how to enhance the bat's exposure. I had already voiced my frustrations to the company, and verbally had given them suggestions on how to improve sales. But no changes were made.

Finally, after numerous discussions and telephone conferences, I told them I wanted out of the contract. There was an "out" clause available to either party if there was any dissatisfaction. That's why I found no harm in originally signing with them. But now, I was very unhappy and finally terminated my contract. It was confirmed by follow up letters by Tom. They acknowledged everything had come to an end. It was over.

After terminating the contract, other companies started to make me offers. By that time, I had made the Olympic team, and suddenly the market potential was booming. Three weeks later I had decided to sign with Louisville Slugger. Tom notified my previous bat company just as a sign of good faith. One week later, I received a letter in the mail informing me that I was being sued.

I was stunned. It all boiled down to money, of course. They wanted to prevent me from having other opportunities.

Lisa was right. I can't emphasize enough the need to secure proper, trustworthy representation before you sign any sort of contract.

I felt badly for Tom because he'd had nothing to do with this contract, but now he was spending the majority of his time trying to solve it. Many months passed before the suit was settled, but the damage was done. I lost a number of endorsement possibilities as the lawsuit scared off prospective companies.

Nevertheless, Tom and I secured an agreement with Rawlings® Sporting Goods. Not only was I to be the first female athlete they'd ever endorsed, but I was given the opportunity to design my own glove.

At first, I explained it over the phone to Bob Clevenhagan, the "King Glove Maker of the World." I wanted a "double break" in the palm so I wouldn't always have to fight the tendency of the glove to malform. This created a much better pocket. Then I suggested to put the finger stalls closer together to accommodate smaller sized hands. Also, I suggested a different location for the finger straps, allowing adjustments that resulted in improved closure of the glove.

I faxed the drawing of the design and my hand print to assist in making the glove. Bob designed it to perfection. When I discovered that Ken Griffey, Jr.'s glove was black with brown lacing, I immediately decided that I wanted my glove to have the same look. Most importantly, Rawlings was willing to listen to my input when it came time to manufacture the product.

It hasn't been easy to see male athletes signing seven or eight figure contracts while women athletes get only a fraction of that. I see male high school basketball players who have just graduated, earning ten million dollars off endorsements. In terms of marketability, I often wonder what a man with my athletic pedigree would earn: fourteen time All-American, four time collegiate All-American, four time World Champion, four time Pan-American, Olympic gold medalist, and a medical degree thrown in for good measure.

Sometimes, Tom becomes frustrated when corporations underestimate the size of the softball market. He'll explain that when I do a clinic, there are five hundred coaches and four hundred and fifty kids. I can go all over the country and do clinics like that nearly every weekend. That's how popular the sport is.

The challenge is balancing that drive to earn recognition, both for yourself and your sport, with the goals and needs of your team and teammates. That has been an important part of what Tom has done for me. He has asked a number of the products I've endorsed to provide free gear for the entire team I was playing on. And in each case, they've done it. That has allowed my teammates to see the benefits from some of the good things that have happened in my life.

Having a man as an agent has, I think, been an eye opening experience for both of us. He has had to go through the struggles that we as women are going through. He represents us and sees that the dollar figures offered to us are nowhere near what's offered to his male clients.

While some may be troubled by the presence of agents in our sport, and fear that it is becoming more commercialized, I'm glad to see it happen. Athletes need that assistance. I have a six-figure debt due to education costs and barely earn enough to pay my day-to-day expenses. This was after four years of undergraduate college, two and a half years of masters study, four years of medical school, and three years at my residency. I couldn't survive without corporate support.

Tom and I have been extremely selective about the companies we've chosen to sign endorsement contracts with. In each case, we've carefully examined the corporation's commitment to both the sport of softball and female athletics in general.

I sincerely believe that we are on the threshold of a huge shift in the perception of women athletics. All of the companies that I have chosen to endorse are at the forefront of advancing this cause; I do not hesitate in saluting the efforts of Bausch & Lomb, Coca-Cola, Flexall, IGA, Inc., Louisville Slugger, Perfect Practice Gear, Rawlings® Sporting Goods, and Reebok International Ltd. for their generous assistance not only to me, but also to female athletics in general. Together, we have increased the opportunities and opened the doors for those who follow.

CHAPTER

FOURTEEN

Final Words

A day does not go by, no matter how hectic my hospital schedule may be, in which I forget to pause and thank God for all the wonderful opportunities He has given me. I've been blessed with so much in my lifetime. Each day I bound from my bed, ready to meet new challenges and learn the day's lessons.

With this book, it was my goal to impart much of what I've learned in my thirty-five years of life. Yet there are intangibles that, try as I may, I can never truly share them. The feeling of the hard infield beneath my cleats. The sense of the ball popping into my well-oiled glove for the millionth time. Watching a little girl's face light up as I place an Olympic gold medal around her neck. Powerful emotions that must be experienced for oneself.

Of all that I have learned, perhaps the most important lesson is to never underestimate the potential of the human mind. It shouldn't come as a surprise that this final thought was illustrated to me through one of the dreams I had as a young girl. And like so many dreams before it, this one took place on the softball field. . . .

I was at my normal position at shortstop when a hard, ground ball was hit right up the middle of the infield. Resolved to make the play, I dug in and ran as fast as I could to try to get in front of it. I sensed that I wouldn't reach the ball in time, but as a final act of determination, I dove headfirst. Stretching my arm out to its full extension, I felt the ball thud solidly into the pocket of my glove. The momentum of my dive launched me into a forward roll, and I came out of the maneuver solidly on my feet. My throw to first base was deadly accurate, and the runner was called out.

In my opinion, any dream in which I'm making plays like that is an incredible dream, and I enjoyed the recurrence of this particular one for almost two years.

But to my amazement and shock the dream became complete one night when I was playing the second game of a doubleheader. It all began to unfold. Literally, I lived this vision exactly as I'd dreamt it. The ground ball up the middle. The dive. The catch. The forward roll. The out.

The thirty-five hundred people in the grandstands broke into thunderous applause. The place was in total pandemonium. My teammates gave each other high-fives. As for myself, I just stood there frozen. I had never practiced such a play; the only preparation I'd had was in dreaming it over the past twenty-four months. I had just lived the dream.

And for the first time in my life, I realized the power of the mind. That if I could imagine it, if I was willing to work so hard for it, that I even dream about it, then it can happen.

I know that if I can live my dreams, then so can you.

TRIBUTE TO THE DREAM

For three long years, the finest women softball players in the country went through the arduous process of trying out for the 1996 United States Olympic Softball team. Through the three different levels of camps all the way down to the final tryouts, the selection committee was given the unenviable task of choosing just fifteen players and five alternates to represent the United States at the Centennial Games. Those women selected were Laura Berg, Gillian Boxx, Sheila Cornell, Lisa Fernandez, Michele Granger Paulos, Lori Harrigan, Dionne Harris, Kim Maher, Leah O'Brien, Dot Richardson, Julie Smith, Michelle Smith, Shelly Stokes, Dani Tyler, and Christa Williams, with the five alternates being Jennifer Brundage, Barbara Jordan, Jennifer McFalls, Martha O'Kelly, and Michelle Venturella.

That only twenty women could be chosen ultimately meant that many others, equally deserving, would be left behind. On the morning the team was announced, the celebration of those players selected was short-lived, as we realized the immense depth of talent among the women who hadn't made the team. More than anything about that moment, I clearly recollect the pain and disappointment that was etched on the faces of so many.

I remember seeing Suzy Brazney dejectedly packing her suitcase to fly home. A fellow All-American, Suzy had been playing softball about as long as I had. Jill Justin and Pat Dufficy, two outstanding players who were my Brakette teammates, also were not chosen. I couldn't believe that Jill wouldn't be playing with us, as I'd felt certain that she would make the squad. When I attempted to comfort her, she and I simply embraced through a flood of shared tears.

Also, I remember Martha O'Kelly collapsing into the arms of National Team Director Cindy Bristow. Though she'd been named as an alternate, Martha was devastated over her sorrow that Jenny Condon hadn't made the team. Martha was not alone in her grief; we found ourselves doing very little rejoicing, as most of our emotion was spent in consoling those who hadn't been so fortunate.

There was such a bond among the women who had worked so long and hard; we were all striving to live an Olympic dream. For those of us who were chosen, we felt a definite, certain responsibility to succeed in the Centennial Games. We simply *had* to win the gold medal; we owed it as tribute to those exceptional women who couldn't be with us.

We were chosen to represent you. We hope you felt it through us. And mostly, we hope we made you proud.